Accent on Science

Authors

Dr. Robert B. Sund
University of Northern Colorado
Dr. Donald K. Adams
University of Northern Colorado
Dr. Jay K. Hackett
University of Northern Colorado
Dr. Richard H. Moyer
University of Michigan–Dearborn

Charles E. Merrill Publishing Co.
A Bell and Howell Company
Columbus, Ohio
Toronto, London, Sydney

Consultants

Content Consultants
Jeanne Bishop, Parkside Junior High, Westlake, OH
York Clamann, Abilene Ind. School District, Abilene, TX
Lucy Daniel, Rutherfordton-Spindale High School, Rutherfordton, NC
Annette Saturnelli, Marlboro Schools, Marlboro, NY
Robert Smoot, McDonogh School, McDonogh, MD
Reading Consultant
Richard Rezba, Virginia Commonwealth University, Richmond, VA
Safety Consultant
Franklin D. Kizer, Council of State Science Supervisors, Lancaster, VA
Special Needs Consultant
Janet Mansfield Davies, Boulder, CO

A Merrill Science Program

Accent on Science, Pupils' Editions, K–6, and Teachers' Editions, K–6
Accent on Science, Poster Cards, K
Accent on Science, Teacher Resource Books (Reproducible Masters), 1–6
Accent on Science, Evaluation and Activity Programs (Spirit Duplicating Masters), 1–6
Accent on Science, Activity Books, 1–6, and Teachers' Annotated Editions, 1–6

Authors

Dr. Robert B. Sund was Professor of Science Education at the University of Northern Colorado. Dr. Sund's teaching experience spanned the elementary through college levels. His many graduate students continue to be active in providing quality science education for today's students. Dr. Sund served as a department head and as a consultant to many school districts as well as to many professional science and mathematics teachers' organizations. As author or coauthor of over twenty professional books, including *Teaching Science Through Discovery, Teaching Modern Science, Creative Questioning and Sensitive Listening Techniques,* and *Piaget for Educators,* he is recognized internationally.

Dr. Donald K. Adams is Professor of Education and Director, Education Field Experiences at the University of Northern Colorado. He holds a B.S. in Liberal Arts Social Science, an M.S. in Biological Science, and an Ed.D in Science Education with support in Earth Science. He has been instrumental in implementing personalized science and outdoor education programs for students in kindergarten through college. With over 20 years of teaching experience, he has served as a consultant to teacher preparation programs and science programs throughout the United States, Australia, and New Zealand.

Dr. Jay K. Hackett is Professor of Earth Science Education at the University of Northern Colorado. He hold a B.S. in General Science, an M.N.S. in Physical Science, and an Ed.D in Science Education with support in Earth Science. A resource teacher for elementary schools, he conducts numerous workshops and professional seminars. With over 20 years of teaching experience, he has taught and consulted on science programs from the elementary to the college level and remains active in local, state, and national science professional organizations.

Dr. Richard H. Moyer is Associate Professor of Science Education at the University of Michigan, Dearborn. He holds a B.S. in Chemistry and Physics Education, an M.S. in Curriculum and Instruction, and an Ed.D in Science Education. With more than 15 years of teaching experience at all levels, he is currently involved in teacher training and environmental education. He is the 1983 recipient of the University of Michigan, Dearborn Distinguished Faculty Award and is a member of Michigan's State Science Superintendant's Committee. He conducts numerous workshops and inservice training programs for science teachers and has authored an enviornmental attitude assessment instrument that has been used extensively for research purposes.

Reviewers: Teachers and Administrators
Thomas Custer, Old Mill Senior High School, Annapolis, MD
Sandra Eliason, Country Side Elementary School, Edina, MN
J. Thomas Fangman, New Providence High School, New Providence, NJ
Tom Hayes, North City Elementary School, Seattle, WA
Frank Mondi, Margate Middle School, Margate, FL
Edward Ortleb, St. Louis Public Schools, St. Louis, MO
Roger Spratt, Ames Community Schools, Ames, IA
Juanita Sutterfield, Oakland Heights Elementary School, Russellville, AR
Nancy Thornton, Central Institute for the Deaf, St. Louis, MO

Cover Photo: Spinner dolphins in sea at sunset by © Robert Hernandez / Photo Researchers

Series Editor: Karen S. Allen; *Project Editor:* Jane L. Parker; *Book Design:* William Walker; *Project Artist:* Michael T. Henry; *Artist:* Jeanine S. Means; *Illustrators:* Jim Robison, Bert Dodson; *Photo Editors:* Lindsay Gerard, Elaine Comer; *Production Editor:* Annette Hoffman; *Paper Sculpture:* Blake Hampton

ISBN 0-675-06845-2

Published by
Charles E. Merrill Publishing Company
A Bell & Howell Company
Columbus, Ohio 43216

Table of Contents

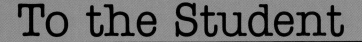

To the Student

Science is an important part of your life and your world. ACCENT ON SCIENCE will help you see how much science is a part of your life and your world.

You will seek and explore many parts of your world. ACCENT ON SCIENCE will show you how scientists study the world. You will find answers to questions such as: How can animals and plants be grouped? What causes seasons? What is known about space? How are forces and motion important to you?

I will guide you through your adventure. We will discover many new and exciting ideas. I hope you will learn some science on your own. Turn the page and let us begin.

2

Animals in the Environment

Chapter One
Animals with Backbones

How many animals can you name? How are some animals alike? Where would you see a lot of different animals? How could you group them?

If you go to a zoo, how would you find the birds? How would you find the fish? You would need a zoo map. The map would show where certain animals could be found. Birds may be found in the bird house. Some birds may be found in an outside cage. Animals are placed in groups at the zoo. How does this grouping help you find the animals you want to see?

Classifying Animals

There are many kinds of animals in our environment. Scientists classify animals. Scientists use classifying to group the many kinds of animals. Classifying helps keep order and makes it easier for people to identify and to learn about animals. **Classifying** is a way to group by using certain characteristics. One characteristic for classifying animals might be a body part. What body parts do you and the animals on the opposite page have in common?

Scientists use a characteristic to classify animals into two groups. The characteristic is a backbone. Animals with backbones are called **vertebrates** (VURT uh brayts). Animals without backbones are called **invertebrates** (in VURT uh brayts).

The animals you see pictured above include vertebrates and invertebrates. Animals such as jellyfish, clams, and insects are examples of invertebrates. You may have observed vertebrates in zoos or on farms. Fish are vertebrates that live in the water. Cats are vertebrates that live on land. You are a vertebrate because you have a backbone. Both you and a cat are similar land vertebrates. How are you like a cat? How are fish different from cats?

Scientists think vertebrates are more complex animals than invertebrates. Vertebrates have more body parts, and the parts are more complex. Invertebrates have few, simple body parts. Compare the animals in the picture above. Some are invertebrates and some are vertebrates. What differences can you see? Which are vertebrates? Which are invertebrates?

Classifying animals is like putting together jigsaw puzzles. Some puzzles, like the simple invertebrates, have few pieces or body parts. They are easy to put together or group. Other puzzles, like the complex vertebrates, have many pieces or body parts. They are more difficult to put together or group.

Each vertebrate has a skeleton inside its body. A **skeleton** is a structure that gives shape and support to an animal's body. The skeleton also protects the inside body organs. Place your hand on your lower back. Feel your backbone. Bend over and straighten up. Do this several times. Feel how your backbone moves as you move. Feel your ribs. How do the backbone and ribs protect the inside parts of your body? What other inside body parts does your skeleton protect?

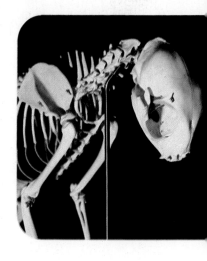

Scientists classify vertebrates into five main groups. They are fish, amphibians (am FIHB ee unz), reptiles (REP tilez), birds, and mammals. Each group has characteristics different from the other groups. The animals are grouped from simple to complex. For example, fish are a simple group of vertebrates. Amphibians are more complex than fish. Reptiles do not have as simple organs as fish or amphibians. Birds are more complex than reptiles. Mammals are the most complex vertebrates.

Fish

Fish are the simplest group of vertebrates. They are also the largest group of vertebrates. All fish have similar characteristics. They all have skeletons. Most of the fish you have seen have skeletons made of bone. A few have skeletons made of cartilage (KART ul ihj).

Cartilage is a firm, flexible substance that forms parts of some skeletons. Sharks and rays have cartilage instead of bone. Your body has both bone and cartilage. Feel the tip of your nose. Wiggle it. Compare the tip of your nose to the upper part of your nose. How does the cartilage feel? Where else on your head can you feel cartilage?

Fish also have scales. **Scales** are thin, smooth pieces of a bonelike material that cover the entire body of the fish. Each scale overlaps another scale. The tough, hard scales help protect fish. How are the scales like a coat of armor?

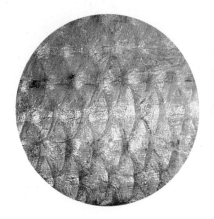

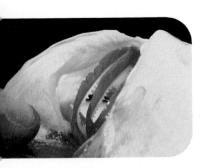

Fish live in water. **Gills** are organs through which fish get oxygen from the water. You can see the gills on the side of the fish's head through the openings or slits. As water enters the mouth, it passes over the gills. Oxygen in the water moves into the gills. Carbon dioxide from the body is given off through the gills. The water then passes out of the body through the slits. Find the slits visible on the fish in the pictures. The gills are beneath the slits.

Fish are cold-blooded animals. **Cold-blooded animals** have a body temperature the same as their environment. For example, fish living in warm water have a warm body temperature. Fish living in cold water have a cold body temperature.

Most fish have fins which are bony limbs covered with thin skin. Fish use fins and body movements to move through the water. Count the fins on the fish. How many does it have? Where are the fins located?

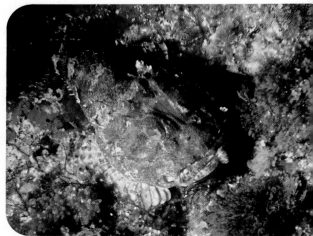

Most fish lay eggs into a nest on the bottom of a pond, stream, or ocean. The eggs hatch into small fish. Some fish, such as guppies, give birth to live young instead of laying eggs.

There are many fresh and saltwater fish. Look at the fish in the top pictures. What characteristics do they have? How are they different? Which looks like a snake? Which looks like a rock?

The simplest fish is the lamprey (LAM pray). Like sharks and rays, lampreys have cartilage skeletons instead of bone skeletons. The lamprey's teeth form a circle inside its mouth. It has no upper or lower jaw. To eat, it holds onto another fish. The sharp teeth of the lamprey cut through the fish's scales and the lamprey sucks blood from the fish.

Lampreys on fish

Lamprey's mouth

It can be fun to observe and learn about fish! The behavior of some fish is unusual. Some fish can leap out of the water and glide through the air. The walking catfish uses its side and tail fins to crawl on land from one body of water to another. The mouthbreeder hides its young in its mouth to protect them from danger. When danger has passed, the mouthbreeder spits the young back into the water. How does this action help the young fish survive?

Fish are important to us. They can provide us with recreation and food. They can provide us with hours of enjoyment as pets. What kinds of fish do you like to eat? Parts of fish can be used for cat and dog food. Other parts of fish can be used in making glue. What ways do you use fish?

Amphibians

What animals live part of their lives in water but are not fish? You may have observed tadpoles in the water. They look and act like fish. The young of frogs, toads, and some salamanders are called tadpoles. Frogs, toads, and salamanders are amphibians. **Amphibians** are cold-blooded vertebrates that live part of their lives in water and part of their lives on land.

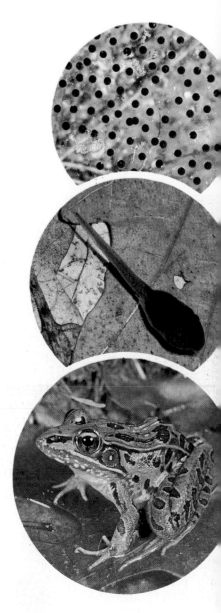

Most amphibians lay eggs in water or in moist places. The eggs are surrounded by a jellylike substance. Tadpoles hatch from the eggs. Notice how the tadpole looks like a small fish. Tadpoles swim and live in the water. They have gills and obtain oxygen from the water. Slowly the tadpoles change. Lungs form inside their bodies as gills disappear. Legs form as fins disappear. Scientists classify amphibians as more complex than fish. Unlike fish, adult amphibians are able to live on land and breathe air.

Adult amphibians look very different from each other. Salamanders have long, thin bodies with tails. Frogs and toads have short front legs and large hind legs. Neither frogs nor toads have tails as adults. Frogs live in or near water. Their skin feels moist and smooth. Toads live mostly on land. Their skin feels dry and rough. Look at the pictures on this page. How do you know which is a frog?

Amphibians are an important part of the environment. They eat flies, mosquitoes, and other insects. Why are their eating habits useful to people? Some people enjoy eating frog legs. They think the meat tastes like chicken but a little sweeter. What other ways are amphibians useful to people?

Reptiles

Another group of vertebrates is reptiles. **Reptiles** are vertebrates that have dry, scaly skin. Like fish and amphibians, reptiles are cold-blooded animals. Alligators, crocodiles, lizards, snakes, and turtles are reptiles.

Unlike fish and amphibians, most reptiles live all of their lives on land. They do not lay eggs in the water. Reptiles lay their eggs on land. The eggs have tough, protective shells. The eggs are covered with sand or soil. As sun warms the cover, the eggs hatch into small adultlike reptiles. The young reptiles are able to find food and move by themselves. They do not change form like amphibians.

Reptiles have well-developed lungs. Even very young reptiles use their lungs to breathe. Scientists think the well-developed lungs make reptiles more complex than fish and amphibians. Reptiles also have more complex hearts than fish and amphibians.

The outer body parts of reptiles look different. Lizards have legs and feet but snakes do not. Turtles have a hard shell used for protection. How is an alligator different from a snake or a turtle?

People should treat some reptiles with caution. Certain snakes can be dangerous. Many reptiles can be harmful if they are threatened. What can you do to prevent a reptile bite?

Reptiles are important to our environment. Farmers welcome some snakes in their gardens and barns because they eat rodents and insects. Some people also enjoy observing and caring for reptiles as pets. Why should reptiles not be harmed?

Making Sure

1. What characteristic is used by scientists to classify an animal as a vertebrate?
2. How is a reptile more complex than an amphibian?

Birds

Vertebrates with feathers for a body covering are called **birds.** Look around your school. What birds do you see? You may see songbirds. There are many different kinds of birds in our environment. Birds, like the hummingbird, can be as small as five centimeters long. The ostrich, however, is over two meters tall. What size are most birds?

Some characteristics of birds are similar to fish, amphibians, and reptiles. All of these animals are vertebrates and lay eggs. However, birds' eggs have a hard outer shell like some reptile eggs. Birds breathe through lungs like adult amphibians and reptiles. Some birds live on land and on water. What can some birds do that some other animals cannot? What birds do not fly? What birds can swim?

Activity

How Can Birds Fly?

What to use:

chicken bones   hand lens
beef or pork bones   pencil and paper

What to do:

1. Have your teacher break the chicken bones apart.

2. Use a hand lens to observe the insides of the chicken bones. Draw a picture of the insides.

3. Observe the cut edges of the beef or pork bone. Draw a picture of the inside of the bone.

4. Compare the two pictures.

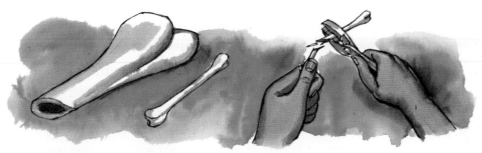

What did you learn?

1. How were the chicken bones different from the beef or pork bone?
2. Which bones were heavier? Which were bigger?
3. Which bones make the best skeleton for flying?

Using what you learned:

1. If you were blindfolded and held a chicken bone and a beef bone of the same size, how would you know which belongs to an animal that flies?
2. What ideas have people gained from learning about birds?

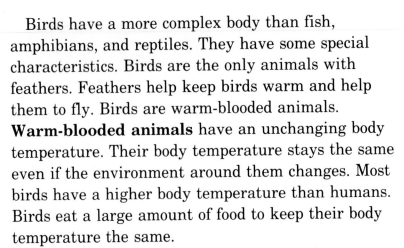

Birds have a more complex body than fish, amphibians, and reptiles. They have some special characteristics. Birds are the only animals with feathers. Feathers help keep birds warm and help them to fly. Birds are warm-blooded animals. **Warm-blooded animals** have an unchanging body temperature. Their body temperature stays the same even if the environment around them changes. Most birds have a higher body temperature than humans. Birds eat a large amount of food to keep their body temperature the same.

Most birds care for their young while fish, amphibians, and reptiles do not. You may have observed birds sitting on their eggs in nests. Why do you think the eggs need to be kept warm? When the eggs hatch, the adult birds must feed the young and protect them.

Since birds are warm-blooded animals, they may live in more than one kind of environment. Penguins (PEN gwunz) are birds that live in cold, snowy areas.

Some colorful birds, such as parrots, are found in warm areas. Other birds live in areas where the temperature changes with the seasons. When the temperature changes with the seasons, the birds will migrate, or fly, to live in a warmer area.

Many people enjoy birds in different ways. Some birds such as chickens, ducks, and turkeys are used for food. Their eggs are also good to eat. Birds can be fun to learn about because many have interesting habits. Birds can be fun to care for as pets. Some birds have beautiful songs. Which birds have colorful feathers? The feathers of some birds are used for pillows, blankets, clothing, and sleeping bags. Birds eat insects and other pests. How else are birds useful?

Mammals

You may know many kinds of animals that have fur. Your pets may have fur. If you have a pet with fur, you have a mammal. **Mammals** are vertebrates with fur or hair. Female mammals can produce milk for their young. Scientists classify mammals as the most complex animals.

The characteristics of mammals are more like birds than amphibians or reptiles. Both birds and mammals care for and protect their young. Both groups are warm-blooded animals and have special body coverings to keep them warm. What are the special coverings of birds and mammals?

Mammals are different from birds and other vertebrates in some ways. Most mammals do not lay eggs. The eggs of most mammals grow and change inside the mother. Most young mammals are born alive. Young mammals get milk from their mothers. Some are cared for longer than the young of birds.

Another difference between mammals and other vertebrates is the brain. A mammal has a more complex brain than other animals. A complex brain is one reason scientists classify people as the highest form of mammals. People can think about and solve very difficult problems. People can use their hands in advanced ways. They can hold objects with their hands, use them as tools, and do other difficult tasks.

There are many kinds of mammals. Elephants and whales are large mammals. Shrews and mice are small mammals. Mammals live almost everywhere.

Monkeys, squirrels, and tree sloths live in trees. Whales, dolphins (DAHL funz), and manatees (MAN uh teez) are mammals which spend their lives in water. Bats are mammals that fly. Moles and gophers are mammals that live underground.

Some mammals have very special body parts. Kangaroos have a special pouch. The mother carries her young in this pouch. It gives protection and warmth to the young. What other animals have a pouch? What special body parts do giraffes, opossums (uh PAHS umz), and porcupines have?

Some mammals can be harmful. Others are important to our environment. Rats and mice carry disease and eat and destroy our food. All animals have a place in the food chain. People benefit from some mammals like sheep, cows, pigs, and rabbits. These mammals are raised for food and fur. The shaggy fur of the alpaca (al PAK uh) can be made into soft, warm sweaters. People like to have some mammals as pets. What mammals make good pets? You can observe and learn about other mammals in zoos or wildlife parks.

Characteristics for Classifying

Scientists observe other characteristics of animals to classify them. For example, a rat has a backbone, so it is classified as a vertebrate. It also has fur and when it is young, it drinks milk from its mother. It is a mammal. The rat has sharp front teeth used for gnawing. Because of the special teeth, rats are classified into a group of mammals called rodents. The rat is a vertebrate, mammal, rodent. How would you classify a bear?

No Milk Today?

Milk is never an item on our family's grocery list. That is because my sister and I have two pet goats. Each of our goats gives about four liters of milk a day. Goats' milk tastes good and it is good for you, too. There are more people in the world who drink goats' milk than cows' milk. We also make cheese and yogurt from our goats' milk.

My sister and I have two does. Does are female goats. Male goats are called bucks. Some people call does "nanny goats" and bucks "billy goats." Baby goats are called kids. My sister's goat is named Lilly and my goat is named Rosie. Our goats come to us when we call their names. Lilly and Rosie are friendly. They like to have people pet them.

Our goats are playful and curious. They follow us around and play games with us in the yard. We have a fence around our yard to keep our goats from wandering away. The fence is almost two meters high because goats are good jumpers and climbers.

Goats need special care. They eat hay and grain. Carrots are a special treat for Lilly and Rosie. My sister and I give our goats plenty of fresh water to drink, too. Each day we brush their fur and milk them. We spend a lot of time caring for our goats, but we think they are worth it. They give us good food and friendship in return.

Chapter Review

Summary

- Grouping animals with certain characteristics is classifying.
- Animals with backbones are vertebrates.
- Animals without backbones are invertebrates.
- Fish have gills and scales and live in water.
- Amphibians are vertebrates that live part of their lives in water and part of their lives on land.
- Reptiles are cold-blooded animals with dry, scaly skin.
- Birds are warm-blooded animals with feathers.
- Mammals are warm-blooded animals with fur or hair.

Science Words

classifying	scales	reptiles
vertebrates	gills	birds
invertebrates	cold-blooded	warm-blooded
skeleton	animals	animals
fish	amphibians	mammals
cartilage		

Questions

1. Why do scientists classify animals?
2. Into what two groups are all animals classified?
3. What are three characteristics of fish?
4. How do scales protect fish?
5. What are tadpoles?
6. How are amphibians able to live in water and on land?
7. How are reptiles more complex than amphibians?
8. How do snakes and turtles differ from other reptiles?
9. How are reptiles important in our environment?
10. How are birds more complex than reptiles?
11. How are mammals more complex than other vertebrates?
12. What group of mammals has the most complex brain?

Chapter Two
Animals without Backbones

What animals are invertebrates? What invertebrates might you observe in a garden? What invertebrates might you observe in the classroom?

$\mathbf{A}$nimals without backbones are called invertebrates. The bodies of invertebrates, such as snails, insects, and worms are not as developed or as complex as vertebrates. Yet, invertebrates are as important as vertebrates. The invertebrates are a part of the food chain and each one is useful in the environment.

Classifying Invertebrates

Invertebrates are found everywhere in our environment. Because there are so many of them, scientists classify them into groups. In this way, it makes it easier to identify each kind of invertebrate. Classifying or grouping helps to keep order.

How do scientists classify invertebrates? Scientists classify vertebrates by considering the characteristics of each group. Invertebrate groups are also classified from simple to complex according to characteristics of the body parts. The invertebrate groups from simple to complex are the sponges, hollow-bodied animals, worms, mollusks (MAHL usks), arthropods (AR thruh pahdz), and spiny-skinned animals. You may already be able to name some invertebrates in each of these groups.

23

Sponges

Look at these sponges. What do they look like to you? Do not confuse invertebrate sponges with sponges made by people. Invertebrate sponges live in water. Most live in groups on the ocean bottom.

Sponges are the simplest invertebrates. Sponges have no special organs or body parts for digesting food and getting oxygen from the water. The bodies of sponges contain many holes. The holes lead to the center of the body where water carries food and oxygen. Sponges use the oxygen and food from the water. Sponge wastes flow out through one or more larger holes in the body.

Some people think sponges look like plants. Adult sponges attach to objects in the water such as rocks. Sponges cannot make their own food like plants. They must get their food like other animals. Sponges are not plants. They are simple invertebrates.

Sometimes people who gather sponges may cut them in half. One part is kept. The part of the sponge thrown back into the water will attach itself to an object and regenerate (rih JEN uh rayt). Animals that **regenerate** can regrow missing body parts. One sponge cut into parts can regenerate the missing parts.

Sponges also form new sponges by growing buds. After a bud is formed on a sponge, it drops off and attaches itself to an object.

People can use some sponges to wash cars, pots, and other objects. Divers collect sponges from the ocean bottom and allow them to dry. Only the soft, spongy skeleton remains when the sponges are washed and dried. The soft part is the part of the sponge you use.

Hollow-Bodied Animals

Jellyfish, hydra, coral, and sea anemones (uh NEM uh neez) make up another group of simple invertebrates. They are hollow-bodied animals. **Hollow-bodied animals** are invertebrates with a hollow center and only one opening.

In some ways, hollow-bodied animals are like sponges. Hollow-bodied animals live in water, and some look like plants. Some hydra, some sea anemones, and most coral attach themselves to rocks or the ocean floor. Others, like jellyfish, float or swim in the water. These hollow-bodied animals can regrow missing body parts. What do we call the ability to regrow body parts?

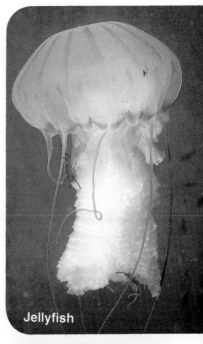
Jellyfish

Sea anemone

Hydra

25

Jellyfish with prey

Scientists consider hollow-bodied animals more complex than sponges. Hollow-bodied animals have one large opening or mouth. Water and food go in and out of the mouth. This mouth is a more complex body part than the many pores of sponges.

Look at the tentacles (TENT ih kulz) around the mouth of the jellyfish. Tentacles are fingerlike parts that are used to bring food into the mouth. Some tentacles are very long. The stingers on the jellyfish tentacles may shock or kill small animals for food. The stingers can also protect the jellyfish from predators. Why is it dangerous to touch a jellyfish?

Hydras and sea anemones have short tentacles. The tentacles look like the petals of a flower as they wave in the water and capture food. Some people think hydras and sea anemones are plants because they grow on rocks on the ocean floor.

Unlike hydras and sea anemones, coral lives in large groups or colonies. Coral may look like tree branches, organ pipes, or beads. People use coral in different ways. How have you seen coral used?

26

Worms

Worms are soft-bodied invertebrates that are classified into three groups. The three worm groups are flatworms, roundworms, and segmented worms. In some ways, worms are like sponges and hollow-bodied animals. Worms can regenerate body parts and some can live in water.

Worms are more complex than sponges and hollow-bodied animals in other ways. Many worms have a head and a body. The body contains many complex organs. Some worms live on land. Others live inside the bodies of animals.

Worms that live inside the bodies of other animals are parasites (PER uh sites). **Parasites** are living things that feed on other living things. When some meat, such as pork, is not cooked long enough, people may get worms by eating the meat. The worms attach themselves to the intestines where they absorb food. Soon people who have parasites may lose weight and become weak. Why is it important to cook meat well?

A flatworm is pictured at the top of this page. Flatworms are the simplest worms. They have one body opening and a digestive system with intestines. Some flatworms are scavengers (SKAV un jurz). **Scavengers** are animals that eat dead animals. The flatworm, planarian (pluh NAR ee un), is a scavenger. Other flatworms are parasites.

Roundworms are more complex than flatworms. They have two body openings, not one. The openings are connected by a long intestine. Food enters the mouth, and wastes leave from the opposite opening.

Segmented worms are the most complex type of worm. Their bodies are divided into small parts, or segments. Two body openings are connected by a long intestine. They have a heartlike organ.

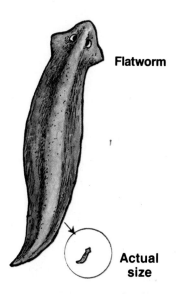

Flatworm

Actual size

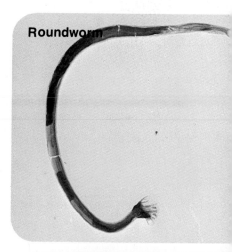

Roundworm

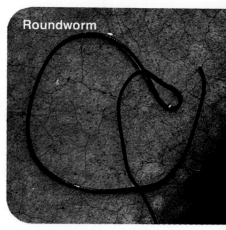

Roundworm

It pumps blood through blood vessels. They even have a small brain in the front part of their bodies. A nerve cord runs the length of their bodies.

Earthworms are important to soil. They make spaces for air and water to enter the soil as they burrow through the soil. The waste from their bodies is also very good for soil. Why are gardeners pleased to have many earthworms in their soil?

Making Sure

1. What are three kinds of invertebrate animals?
2. Name two animals that regenerate.

Mollusks

Mollusks are invertebrates with soft bodies. Many mollusks have shells. Clams, oysters, mussels, and snails are mollusks with hard, outer shells. Sometimes these mollusks are called shellfish. They are not true fish because they lack a backbone, scales, and fins.

Shells are a characteristic of some mollusks. Shells provide protection for the soft bodies of mollusks. Snails, periwinkles, and some slugs have only one shell. Clams, oysters, scallops, and mussels have two shells hinged together on one end. The hinge allows the mollusks' shells to open and close.

Where have you seen slugs and snails? Some mollusks live in fresh or salt water. Some live in moist places on land. You may find some mollusks under leaves and rocks.

The bodies of mollusks are more complex than sponges, hollow-bodied animals, and worms. Mollusks have special body organs for moving, breathing, getting food, and pumping blood. Each organ is for only one function. Special organs for special functions make the mollusks more complex.

The squids and octopuses use their tentacles or arms as feelers to gather food and for protection. Squids have ten arms or tentacles. How many do octopuses have?

Clams, mussels, and snails have a footlike part that can extend out of the shell. The foot is like the tentacles on squids and octopuses. The foot is used for moving, digging, and feeling.

Mollusks are important in our environment. Scallops, oysters, clams, and snails are used for food. Some people like to eat squid and octopus. All mollusks should be cooked well before eating as some mollusks may have parasites.

Activity

What Are the Characteristics of a Snail?

What to use:

snail   water
aquarium (optional)   hand lens
algae   cotton swab
small, flat dish   pencil and paper

What to do:

1. Observe the snails in the aquarium. Find a snail that is eating algae. Use your hand lens to observe.

2. Fill the small, flat dish half-full of water. Have your teacher place the snail and some algae in your dish.

3. Using the hand lens, observe the snail in the dish. Notice how it moves and eats.

4. Draw a picture of the snail.

5. Touch the snail gently with a moist cotton swab. Draw a picture of the snail after you touched it.

What did you learn?

1. What happened when you touched the snail?
2. How is the snail protected by its shell?
3. Describe how the snail moves.

Using what you learned:

1. What is a characteristic of all mollusks?
2. How is a snail like a clam?
3. How is a snail not like a squid?

Arthropods

Arthropods are animals with outer skeletons, jointed legs, and segmented bodies. Three-fourths of all the animals are arthropods. They live all over the Earth. Some live in water and some live on land. Some can fly. How do these arthropods vary in size? What shapes do they have? Arthropods include beetles, bees, crabs, shrimps, spiders, millipedes, and centipedes.

An arthropod is similar to a mollusk because it has an outside skeleton. Yet an arthropod is more complex than other invertebrates because it has body parts that do special jobs. The arthropod's body parts are more complex than the foot and mouth area of a mollusk.

An arthropod's body is divided into sections. Each section has a special job. The head has special mouth parts for holding and chewing food. Several sense organs are on the head for seeing, feeling, tasting, and smelling. The middle and hind body sections have special tubes for breathing.

If you touch an arthropod, you will feel a hard outer skeleton. The animal will molt (MOHLT) its skeleton as it grows. **Molting** is the shedding of the outer skeleton. As the animal grows, it becomes too large for its skeleton. A slit appears along its back, and the arthropod crawls out of its old skeleton. The arthropod has molted its old skeleton. After a short time, a new outside covering forms and becomes hard. Notice the cicada (suh KAYD uh) shown here. How do you know it is molting?

Cicada molting

Millipede

Beetle

Insects are the largest group of arthropods. You have probably seen insects such as aphids, flies, butterflies, and beetles. All adult insects have three pairs of legs. They have eyes and feelers for sensing. Most have wings for flying.

Spiders have four pairs of legs, two body segments, and no wings. Other arthropods classified with spiders are ticks, mites, and scorpions. Some spiders can be dangerous and should not be handled.

Spider

Centipedes and millipedes are wormlike arthropods. They have jointed legs, a head area, and many segments. Centipedes have one pair of legs for each body segment. Millipedes have two pairs of legs for each body segment. Millipedes move slowly in a wavelike motion.

Crabs, crayfish, shrimp, and lobsters are arthropods, too. Their outside skeletons are usually very thick and hard. Their legs are jointed and can bend. Most of these arthropods live in water and use featherlike gills to get oxygen from the water.

Shrimp

Arthropods are important to our world. Some arthropods can be harmful. Insects like the grasshopper and some beetles can ruin plants and food crops. Termites can destroy homes by eating the wooden parts. Roaches and mosquitoes carry disease.

Other arthropods can be helpful for people. Arthropods such as shrimp, crabs, and lobsters are eaten by people. Spiders control the number of insects on Earth by eating them. Insects are a good source of food for other animals, too.

People and Science

Hi, Honey!

When was the last time you ate some honey? You may have eaten some in crackers, bread, or other baked goods. Bakers buy huge amounts of honey to use in their baked goods. They buy the honey from beekeepers. Beekeepers sell about 95 million kilograms of honey each year in the United States. Other honey is sold in small containers for cooking and using as a sweet spread.

Beekeepers nearly always provide hives for their bees. Most hives are like large boxes. Each hive has an outside cover and an inside cover. Sections are put into the hive and taken out of the hive like drawers. The bees build their honeycombs inside the sections. Beekeepers may have as many as 75 hives in one place. Sometimes they move colonies of bees far apart so there are enough plants nearby for nectar.

A colony of bees may gather 11 kilograms of nectar in one day!

Beekeepers seldom get stung by a bee. The beekeepers move carefully and slowly. They wear light-colored clothes which tie at their wrists and ankles. Many beekeepers wear face protection, too.

Beekeepers sell not only the honey but also the beeswax. The beeswax is used in products like candles, lipsticks, and polishes. They also sell or rent the hives of bees to others who want to be beekeepers. Farmers sometimes rent hives so the bees can pollinate their crops. Many people keep bees just to study them because they are easy to handle. Why would you like to be a beekeeper?

Spiny-Skinned Animals

Spiny-skinned animals are animals that have sharp spines on the outsides of their bodies. The sharp spines form a skeleton for protection. Starfish, sand dollars, sea urchins (UR chunz), sea lilies, and sea cucumbers are spiny-skinned animals that live in the ocean.

Tube feet are characteristic of spiny-skinned animals. Tube feet are tiny, suctionlike cups on the underside of these animals. They are used for moving, feeling, and feeding. A starfish uses its tube feet to open the shells of clams or oysters.

Like sponges and worms, starfish can also regenerate. Many years ago, oyster and clam diggers caught starfish and cut them into parts. Thinking the starfish were dead, the parts were thrown back into the ocean. What happened to each part?

Many characteristics of adult spiny-skinned animals are not as complex as arthropods. Spiny-skinned animals, such as starfish, do not have jointed legs. Starfish have stomachs but arthropods have special mouth parts and stomachs. However, the young of spiny-skinned animals have characteristics more complex than the developing young of arthropods.

Characteristics for Classifying

When scientists classify invertebrates, they observe many characteristics. For example, butterflies do not have backbones. Scientists classify butterflies as invertebrates. The segmented bodies and jointed legs place butterflies in the arthropod group. Butterflies have wings and six legs. What group of arthropods has these characteristics? How would you classify spiders and clams?

Chapter Review

Summary

- Sponges are simple invertebrates that can regenerate missing body parts.
- Hollow-bodied animals have tentacles around their mouths.
- Flatworms and roundworms may be scavengers or parasites.
- Mollusks are invertebrates with soft bodies.
- Many mollusks have shells.
- Arthropods have outside skeletons, segmented bodies, and jointed legs.
- Insects are the largest group of arthropods.
- Spiny-skinned animals have sharp spines and tube feet.
- Scientists consider spiny-skinned animals the most complex invertebrates.

Science Words

sponges	worms	arthropods
regenerate	parasites	molting
hollow-bodied animals	scavengers	spiny-skinned animals
	mollusks	

Questions

1. Name the groups of invertebrates from simple to complex.
2. How are segmented worms more complex than squids?
3. How are tube feet used by spiny-skinned animals?
4. In what ways do people use mollusks?
5. Why are parasites unhealthful?
6. What invertebrates are scavengers?
7. How can you avoid getting flatworms and roundworms in your body?
8. Why is being able to regenerate useful to animals?
9. How are arthropods more complex than mollusks?
10. Which arthropods are helpful to the environment?

Self Checks

Answer these Self Checks on a sheet of paper.

1. Copy this chart. Describe each animal group in your chart.

Animal Characteristics			
Animal group	Habitat	Body Covering	Example
Sponges			
Hollow-bodied Animals			
Worms			
Mollusks			
Arthropods			
Spiny-skinned Animals			

2. Identify each vertebrate group shown below.

a

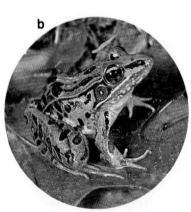
b

c

d

e

💡 Idea Corner
More Fun with Science

1. Draw and label the stages of the development of a frog. If possible, obtain and care for a tadpole, observing the changes which occur.

2. Choose one arthropod and do some research to find out about it. Write or give a report about your choice. Be sure to include its importance to people.

3. Observe a tree nearby. List all the animals that you can see on or near the tree. Classify the animals on your list.

4. Make a bulletin board display of pictures of the products from vertebrates and invertebrates.

Reading for Fun

A First Look at Animals Without Backbones by Millicent Selsam and Joyce Hunt, Walker and Company: New York, © 1976.

    The drawings in this book will help you understand the differences between animals with and without backbones.

Snakes: Their Place in the Sun by Robert M. McClung, Garrard Publishing Company: New Canaan, CT, © 1979.

    The drawings and printed material will help you to learn more about snakes in our environment.

What's in the Names of Wild Animals? by Peter Limburg, Coward, McCann and Geoghegan: New York, © 1977.

    Legends are woven together with this introduction to the classification of animals.

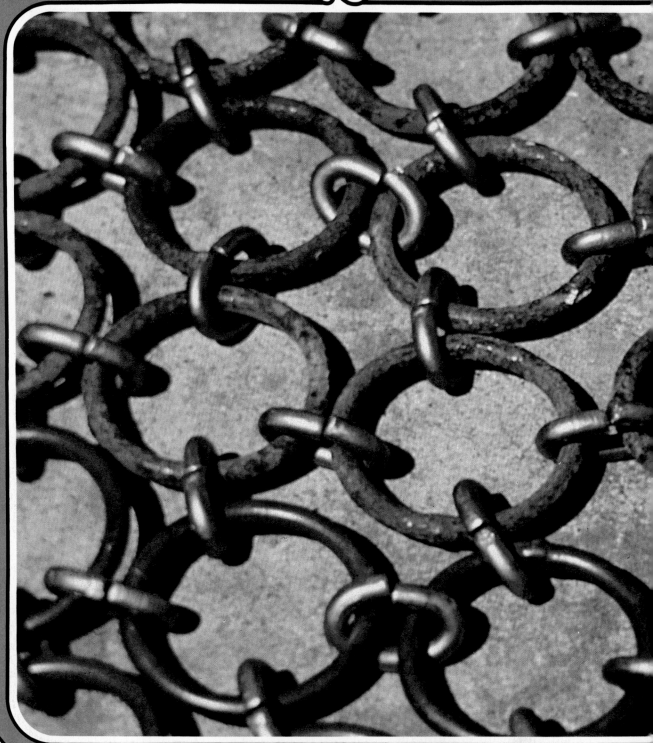

Unit 2

Chapter One

Looking at Matter

What is matter? How do scientists look at different kinds of matter? Where is matter in this picture? What is the smallest part of matter?

Matter is all around you. Your school is matter. Your teacher is matter. You are matter. Everything you see is matter. Some matter, such as air, cannot be seen. **Matter** is a solid, liquid, or gas and takes up space.

The Scientific Method

Sometimes you may wonder what causes an action to happen. You may think of a question but not be sure of an answer. You may want to answer your question by doing an experiment.

Nate wondered what brand of paper towel would absorb the most water. On TV, he heard different companies claim to have the best towels. Nate decided to do an experiment.

Nate collected samples of five different paper towels. By looking at and touching them, Nate found one towel he thought would absorb the most water. He predicted the thickest towel would absorb more water. Next, Nate put each towel into some water. Then he squeezed the water out into a measuring cup, writing how much water each towel held. His experiment showed the thickest towel absorbed the most water.

Nate used the scientific (si un TIHF ihk) method. The **scientific method** is the way scientists solve problems or find answers to questions. You can use the scientific method to solve problems, too.

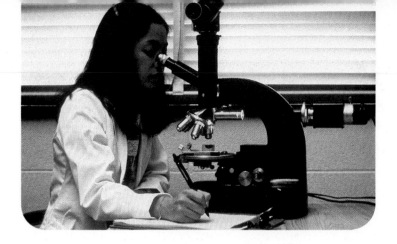

There are many scientific methods because scientists work in many ways. The scientific method most scientists use has five steps. The first step is to state the problem or ask a question. What was Nate's problem?

The second step is to make a prediction. A **prediction** is a guess of what you think may happen. What prediction did Nate make?

The third step is to design and carry out an experiment. An **experiment** is a test to solve a problem or answer a question. It is important to plan and do the experiment carefully. What was Nate's experiment?

Scientists record what they observe while doing an experiment. The fourth step is to record observations. As Nate did his experiment, he wrote what he observed. Why was it important for Nate to record his observations? Observations can be studied and compared to what other scientists observe.

The fifth step is a conclusion. A **conclusion** is a decision or answer to a question. It is made by using the information gained from the experiment. It may solve the problem from step one. What was Nate's conclusion? You may not always be sure of your conclusion. Sometimes the conclusion of an experiment proves the prediction was not correct. Steps two to five must be done again. A new experiment must be designed to test a new prediction.

Often the scientific method is repeated to solve a problem. Scientists find that the conclusions of many experiments raise more questions than are answered. When that happens, more experiments need to be done to try to answer those questions. You can learn new information from the experiments. In Nate's experiment with paper towels, he might ask a new question about the strength of the towels. What other questions might he ask about the paper towels?

You may use the scientific method to answer many questions. You might wonder what affects the growth of plants. You could predict some possible answers. You could design and try some experiments with plants. Suppose you put a plant in a covered box. The box has a hole in the side where light could come through. What would happen? What would happen if you used another kind of plant? You would probably have many more questions. You could do experiments to answer your questions. You could observe and record the results of several experiments.

Making Sure

1. List the five steps in the scientific method.
2. Imagine there are several ways for you to go home from school. Explain how you could use the scientific method to find the fastest way.

Observations

In order to learn more about something, we use our senses to make observations. There are two kinds of observations. Some observations are direct. In a **direct observation,** an object may be both sensed and measured. Nate could see and measure the water absorbed by each towel.

Some matter cannot be sensed or measured. It may be too small or too far away. We learn about this matter through indirect observation. We cannot make direct measurements or use all our senses when making an **indirect observation.**

Scientists must use indirect observations to learn about the inner Earth. By observing volcanoes, they know the inner Earth is very hot. Why is this kind of testing and observing indirect?

Look at the picture above. The boy is saying to the girl, "Oh, I see you have a dog." How did he know the girl had a dog? Is he making a direct or indirect observation?

Indirect observations help us form a model. A **model** explains what cannot be directly observed. Scientists formed a model of the inner Earth. They cannot directly observe the Earth's center. When do you use models in your life?

In the picture, dummies are used to form a model. By observing what happens to dummies in crashes, scientists form a model of what happens to humans in crashes. From the model, safer cars are planned. What other examples of models can you name?

Activity

How Do Scientists Make a Model?

What to use:

mystery box   pencil and paper
wooden stick or pencil

What to do:

1. Tip the box, shake it gently, listen carefully. Use many ways of observation without opening the box. Record your observations.

2. Use the wooden stick to probe or feel the contents of the box. Record your observations.

3. Draw a picture of what you think the contents of the box look like. Share your picture with others.

What did you learn?

1. What ways did you plan to learn the properties of the contents of the mystery box?
2. What observations did you record without using the stick?
3. What observations did you record using the stick?
4. How did your picture compare with others?

Using what you learned:

1. What steps of the scientific method did you use?
2. When did you use direct or indirect observation?
3. How is the picture you drew like the model scientists form?
4. What do scientists need to do before they make models?
5. How might your picture change if you saw the contents of the mystery box?

A Model of Matter

Suppose you could shrink to half your size. How would your desk look to you? Suppose you kept on shrinking. Imagine being as tall as a penny lying on the desk. Stand on your tiptoes and look across the top of the penny. Imagine getting even smaller. What if you could become small enough to walk into the coin. What would you observe inside the penny?

Think of some of the smallest objects you know. What are they? The tiny units that make up matter are even smaller. Scientists call the tiny units atoms. **Atoms** are the building blocks of all matter. They are like bricks in a building. No one can see the atoms in matter. Atoms are too small to observe directly. Scientists must make indirect observations to learn about atoms. By observing the way matter acts, they can form a model of atoms.

Some atoms are found alone. Some atoms combine with other atoms. Two or more atoms joined together in a certain way form **molecules.** Some molecules can be made of two or more of the same kind of atoms. Other molecules are made of different kinds of atoms.

A Molecule of Water

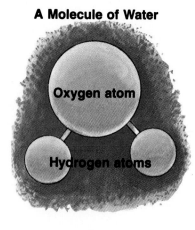

Oxygen atom

Hydrogen atoms

Elements

Silver is a special kind of matter. It is made of only one kind of atom. All the tiny atoms in silver are exactly alike. Matter made of all the same kind of atoms is called an **element.** Silver is an element. Gold is an element, too. Gold atoms are different from silver atoms, but all the atoms in gold are alike.

There are over 100 different elements. That means there are over 100 different kinds of atoms. The atoms that make up each element are different from the atoms of another element.

Elements can be solids, liquids, or gases. Most elements are found as solids in nature. Aluminum is a solid element. It is often used in the home. How is aluminum used by your family? How is aluminum used in your school? Gold and copper are found as solid elements. Many solid elements are found in the Earth in rocks and minerals. How are gold and copper used?

Mercury and bromine (BROH meen) are the only two elements that are found as liquids. CAUTION: Mercury and bromine are very dangerous elements. They should not be handled because they can cause serious illness. Where have you seen mercury used? Bromine is used in fuel for cars and trucks to prevent knocking in engines.

Other elements are found in nature as gases. The element helium is lighter than air. Why do you think helium is used in balloons? Neon is also an element in the gas state. It is often used inside electric signs. Neon gives off a bright red color in signs. Where are these signs used?

Elements are also classified as metals and nonmetals. There are more metallic than nonmetallic elements. Most metals are silver or gray solids. Metals are strong and flexible and can be molded into many shapes. Metals also conduct electricity. What metals do you see in your classroom? How are they used?

Nonmetallic elements are different from metallic elements. Nonmetals do not conduct electricity. They may be in the solid, liquid, or gas state. Solid nonmetals are brittle. They cannot be molded into shapes as easily as metallic elements. Pencil points are made of carbon which is a solid nonmetal. All gases are nonmetals. Air is a mixture of several gases. What nonmetals are in your classroom? How are they used?

Sugar and Spice and . . .

The human body is made of many atoms. The atoms are part of elements, compounds, and mixtures. Oxygen, hydrogen, carbon, and nitrogen are the most common elements in the human body.

The body contains very small amounts of other elements. All the elements are needed for life. If you are missing only one of the elements, you could become very sick. Too much of some elements can also make you sick. A proper balance is needed for good health.

Most of the elements you need are part of the air you breathe, the water you drink, or the food you eat. Some, such as the sodium, chloride, and iodine of table salt, are added to food. Other elements may be obtained as compounds in pills, such as vitamins.

The exact amount of each element in a human body cannot be observed directly. Yet, you can come close to the amount indirectly. The chart shows the amounts of each element in 100 grams of a healthy person. You can find the amount in your body, too.

Amount (g) in 100 g ×
Your mass (g) ÷ 100 =
Amount in you (g)

Element	Amt in 100 g
Oxygen	65 grams
Carbon	18 grams
Hydrogen	10 grams
Nitrogen	3 grams
Other elements	4 grams

Activity

What Are the Properties of Some Compounds?

What to use:

powdered sugar	vinegar
paper cups	eyedropper
water	hand lens
compounds A, B, C, D	pencil and paper

What to do:

1. Make the charts shown below.

Properties of Compounds			
Compound	Sight	Touch	Smell
Sugar			
Compound A			
Compound B			
Compound C			
Compound D			

Properties of Compounds with Vinegar			
Compound	Sight	Touch	Smell
Sugar			
Compound A			
Compound B			
Compound C			
Compound D			

2. Label the cups Sugar, A, B, C, D. Place small samples of each compound in the correct cups.

3. Observe the properties of each. Use sight, touch, and smell to observe the properties of each compound. **Do not taste!** Record your observations on the first chart.

4. Using the eyedropper, add a little vinegar to each sample. Observe and record your observations on the second chart.

What did you learn?

1. In step 3, which compounds were the most alike when observing with your senses?
2. In step 3, which compound was the easiest to observe? Explain why.
3. In step 3, which sense or senses helped you tell the difference between the compounds?
4. In step 4, which compounds were the most alike?
5. In step 4, which compound was the easiest to observe? Explain why.
6. In step 4, which compound or compounds acted the most unusual?
7. What do you think compounds A, B, C, and D are?

Using what you learned:

1. Describe one of your compounds to a classmate. See if the person can guess which compound it is.
2. Try to identify a compound as another classmate describes it to you.
3. What compounds that you know act like one of these compounds when you add vinegar?

Compounds

Most matter around you is not made up of single elements. Water is not an element. Sugar is not an element. Water and sugar are both compounds. **Compounds** are matter made up of more than one kind of element. The elements in compounds are joined together. They cannot be separated easily.

There are many more compounds than elements. In nature, elements may combine to form compounds. Rust is an example. When oxygen in moist air or water combines with iron, rust is formed. You may have seen rust on old cars, bicycles, or other metal objects.

Many useful compounds are formed by scientists. Elements may be combined with other elements to form compounds. Often scientists produce compounds from other compounds. Some foods and most medicines are compounds formed by scientists. Useful fabrics and plastics are formed with compounds present in petroleum and natural gas. We use many compounds in our lives. Each day scientists are able to make new compounds for us to use. Look at the pictures on this page. What compounds can you name? What new compounds have you used? How have they been useful for you?

Properties of elements change when they are combined as compounds. Compounds do not look or act like their separate elements. Each compound has its own different properties. Water is a compound made of the elements hydrogen and oxygen. The properties of both elements are different from the properties of water. Both hydrogen and oxygen are colorless gases. Both have no taste. Hydrogen will burn very quickly in oxygen. Yet, when combined as water, the elements can be seen and felt. What are some properties of water? How do you use water at home and at school?

Chapter Review

Summary

- Matter takes up space and can be solid, liquid, or gas.
- Scientists use the scientific method to find out about matter.
- A model is used to explain what cannot be observed directly.
- Matter is composed of tiny particles called atoms.
- Molecules are made of two or more atoms joined in a certain way.
- Elements are matter made of only one kind of atom.
- Compounds are made of two or more elements that cannot be separated easily.

Science Words

matter	conclusion	atoms
scientific method	direct observation	molecules
prediction	indirect observation	element
experiment	model	compounds

Questions

1. What are the steps in the scientific method?

2. Your mother wants to find out which car wax gives the best shine. Help her use the scientific method to solve her problem. What would you do?

3. How are direct observations different from indirect observations?

4. The sidewalk is wet when you wake up. The grass is wet. You tell your father that it rained last night. What kind of observation did you make?

5. Which forms of matter can you observe directly?
   (a) atoms (c) elements
   (b) molecules (d) compounds

6. How are elements different from compounds? How are they the same?

Chapter Two
Properties of Matter

What do you see around you? How is matter the same? How is matter different? What are some properties of matter?

Not all matter is the same. Matter has different properties. The **properties** of matter are what we can sense or measure. Color, mass, smell, taste, and hardness are some properties of matter. Some of these properties can be sensed. Other properties can be measured. What properties of wet grass can you sense? What properties of wet grass can you measure?

Measuring Matter

One property of matter that can be measured is mass. **Mass** is the amount of matter in an object. All matter has mass, including you. Your mass is how much matter you have in your body.

All matter has mass and takes up space. Solid matter has mass. Liquid and gas matter have mass, too. Mass is measured in **grams** or **kilograms.** Kilo means one thousand. One thousand grams equals one kilogram.

Activity

How Do You Find the Mass of Objects?

What to use:

pan balance   4 five-gram masses
10 checkers   4 one-gram masses
10 coins   pencil and paper

What to do:

1. Make sure the empty scale is balanced. Place the gram masses on the right pan of the balance.

2. Place the 10 checkers on the left pan of the balance.

3. Remove some of the gram masses until the pans are level or balanced. Record the number of gram masses on the right pan.

4. Remove all the checkers from the left pan.

5. Repeat steps 1 through 3. Use the 10 coins in place of the 10 checkers.

What did you learn?

1. How many gram masses remained on the right pan when the checkers balanced?

2. How many gram masses remained on the right pan when the coins balanced?

3. Which has the greater mass, the checkers or the coins?

4. What are you using to compare the checkers?

Using what you learned:

1. How can you find the mass of 20 pennies?

2. How can you find the mass of other small objects in your classroom?

Weight is also a property of matter you can measure. **Weight** is the measure of the amount of pull between objects. Your weight is the measure of pull between the Earth and your body. The pull between the Earth and other objects is gravity.

Since the Earth has more mass than many objects, its pull is greater. It may seem as if only the Earth pulls on objects. Yet, there is a pull between all objects. The amount of pull depends on the mass of the objects. The greater the mass of objects, the greater the pull. The Earth pulls you to the ground when you jump up. What do you think would happen if there were no gravity pulling toward the Earth?

Suppose you go into space, away from the Earth. What would happen to your weight? What would happen to your mass? Imagine you are traveling in a spaceship away from the Earth. There is less pull between the Earth and your body as you move away from Earth. Look at yourself. You still have all of your body. Your mass has not changed. Your weight becomes less if you are farther away from the Earth. Your mass stays the same.

The weight of an object becomes less and less as it moves away from the Earth. The pull or gravity between two objects becomes less as the objects are moved apart. The pull is much like the attraction or pull between two magnets. As the magnets are moved apart, the attraction becomes less and less.

Sir Isaac Newton studied gravity. There is a story that while drinking tea in a garden, Newton saw an apple fall from a tree. He realized that the pull between the Earth and the apple acts the same as the pull between the Earth and the moon. The pull between the Earth and an object is gravity. To honor Newton, the strength of a pull is measured in units called **newtons.** Since weight is a measure of gravity, weight is measured in newtons.

Activity

How Do You Measure Weight?

What to use:

cardboard strip 5 × 30 cm	metric ruler
paper clips	10 large washers
larger, thin rubber band	other small objects
small paper cup	masking tape
wire	pencil and paper

What to do:

1. Copy the chart on page 59.

2. Make a "Puller Pal" like the one shown here.

3. Fasten wire to the paper cup as shown.

4. Hang the cup from the paper clip on the "Puller Pal."

Weighing Objects Chart											
Rubber Band Stretch (mm)	0 mm										
No. of Washers	0	1	2	3	4	5	6	7	8	9	10

5. Make a mark on the "Puller Pal" at the end of the rubber band. Label this mark 0 mm.

6. Add one washer to the paper cup. Make a new mark on the "Puller Pal" at the end of the rubber band. Use a metric ruler to measure the stretch of the rubber band. This is the distance from zero to the new mark. Record the measurement on the chart.

7. Continue adding washers to the cup one at a time. Measure the stretch each time and record the new stretch measurement on the chart.

8. Make a graph of your results.

What did you learn?

1. What was the stretch measurement of the rubber band when one washer was in the paper cup?

2. What happened to the rubber band when more washers were added to the cup?

Using what you learned:

1. Weigh some other objects in your room using the "Puller Pal."

2. Use your graph to predict how far the rubber band may stretch with 20 washers. Try it to see if your prediction was correct.

Matter and Space

You know matter takes up space. Feel your desk. Your desk takes up space. What state of matter is your desk? How many desks could you get into your classroom? The amount of space matter takes up is called **volume.** All matter has volume because all matter takes up space. Volume is a property of matter you can measure.

You would not be able to fill a glass with milk if liquid matter did not take up space. Matter in the gas state also takes up space. How can you be sure air takes up space? The air in a balloon is an example of gas which takes up space. Name other examples.

Measure the length, width, and height of your book. Multiply these numbers together and you will have the volume of your book. Volume equals length times width times height. An eraser is 10 cm tall, 6 cm wide, and 5 cm thick. The volume is

$$10 \text{ cm} \times 6 \text{ cm} \times 5 \text{ cm} = 300 \text{ cubic cm.}$$

Cubic centimeters and cubic meters are units used in measuring volume. A **cube** can be any size, but the length, width, and height of a cube are all the same measure. Look at the cube pictured here. Find the volume of the cube by multiplying the length, width, and height together. Its volume is $1 \text{ cm} \times 1 \text{ cm} \times 1 \text{ cm}$ or one cubic centimeter.

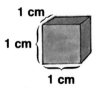

1 cm
1 cm
1 cm

The picture on the right shows how a solid would look if it were divided into cubic centimeters. How many cubic centimeters does it have? How did you find out?

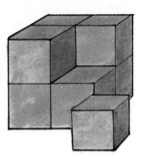

Imagine a cubic container that is 10 cm wide, 10 cm deep, and 10 cm tall. The volume of this imaginary container is

10 cm × 10 cm × 10 cm = 1000 cubic centimeters.

Solids and liquids may both be measured in units of cubic centimeters. However, liquids are usually measured in liters. A liter has the same volume as 1000 cubic centimeters. Imagine that we fill our 1000-cubic cm box with water. The liquid in 1000 cubic cm equals one liter.

The boys in the picture above have a new fish aquarium. It is 70 cm long, 30 cm wide, and 50 cm deep. What is its volume in cubic centimeters? How many cubic centimeters of water can it hold?

Imagine the boys got a larger fish tank. It is 100 cm long, 40 cm wide, and 50 cm deep. What is the volume of the tank? How many cubic centimeters of water can it hold? How many liters?

Making Sure

1. How are mass and weight different?
2. How many liters in 3000 cubic centimeters?
3. How do you find volume?

Density of Matter

Imagine carrying two pails of the same volume. One pail is full of cotton balls. The other pail is full of rocks. Which one would you rather carry a long distance? Why? The pail with rocks has the same volume as the pail with cotton balls. However, the pail with rocks has a greater mass than the pail with cotton. The rocks are harder for you to carry. The density (DEN sut ee) of the rocks is greater than the density of the cotton. **Density** is the amount of mass an object has for its volume. In this example, the rocks have more mass than the same volume of cotton. So the rocks are more dense.

All materials do not have the same density. Compare a golf ball and a ping-pong ball. Which has more mass? Which has more density?

Often the density of objects is compared with water. Objects with a density less than water will float. If the density of the object is greater than water, what will happen to the object? If you mix oil and vinegar for salad dressing, what happens to the oil? Which substance has more density?

Activity

How Do You Measure Density?

What to use:

2 paper cups
popcorn (popped and unpopped)
2 containers of equal size (¼ liter)
water

small bowl
pan balance
pencil and paper

What to do:

1. Fill one of the paper cups with unpopped corn. Fill the other cup with popped corn.

2. Place 1 cup on each pan of the balance. Record which cup has the greater mass.

3. Predict whether the popped or unpopped corn will float in water. Record your predictions.

4. Put some popped and unpopped corn into the bowl with water. Record your observations.

What did you learn?

1. How does the volume of the popped corn compare with the volume of the unpopped corn?

2. Which popcorn has the greater mass?

3. What did you observe when both kinds of popcorn were put in water?

Using what you learned:

1. Does popcorn become more or less dense after it is popped? How do you know?

2. What other foods change in density when they are cooked?

3. Why is popcorn usually sold unpopped rather than popped?

People and Science

Working for Better Metal

What is made of metal? What metal products do you use? Scientists called metallurgists (MET uhl ur juhsts) know how to separate useful metals from rocks. They develop ways to shape metals into the products you use. Many metallurgists work in factories where metal products are made.

Metallurgists make direct observations of the properties of metals. They compare metals by testing different properties. One test is for hardness. Metallurgists test hardness with a machine. The machine measures the dent made in a metal by the pressure of a special ball point.

Some metals that are exposed to air or water will rust. You may have seen rust on an old car. Metallurgists try to find ways to prevent rust. Painting metals is one way to slow the rusting process. Some metals have been improved so that they do not rust easily. Stainless steel is one example. What stainless steel products do you use?

Metallurgists make indirect observations of the atoms in metals. They devise and test theories about the structure of metals. Some metals, such as aluminum, iron, copper, and tin are elements. Other metals are mixtures of two or more elements. These metals are called alloy (AL oi) metals. Steel and brass are alloy metals. Metallurgists know that you want quality metal products. They keep working for ways to improve metals and make new alloys.

Chapter Review

Summary

- Matter has some properties that can be sensed and some that can be measured.
- Mass is the amount of matter in an object.
- Weight is the measure of the amount of gravity between an object and the Earth.
- The attraction between the Earth and other objects is called gravity.
- The amount of space an object takes up is called volume.
- Density is the amount of mass for the volume of matter.

Science Words

properties	**kilograms**	**volume**
mass	**weight**	**cube**
grams	**newtons**	**density**

Questions

1. For which property of matter are each of these used?
   (a) newtons (b) length × width × height (c) kilograms

2. What property of matter can you observe in the following?
   (a) two packages of the same size—one feels heavier than the other
   (b) the amount of pull between the Earth and another object

3. Why do astronauts experience weightlessness in space?

4. You are planning to build a swimming pool.
   (a) What units of measurement would you use to describe the size of the hole you must dig?
   (b) Find how much water you need to fill the pool.

5. Find the volume of water in a tank which is 50 cm high, 20 cm wide, and 50 cm long if
   (a) the tank is full of water. (b) the tank is half full of water.

6. Why do ice cubes float?

Chapter Three
States of Matter

What states of matter do you see here? How does one state change to another? What causes matter to change states? How are properties of each state different?

On a hot summer day you may drink ice water. If you let some of the ice go into your mouth, you will soon notice the ice gets smaller. After awhile there is no ice in your mouth. What happened?

Ice is matter. It is the solid state of water. When ice melts, it becomes a liquid. The ice in your mouth melted, and you were able to swallow it. If the ice melted on the table beside you, it would later change to a gas. Water or any matter can be in a solid state, a liquid state, or a gas state.

Solid Matter

Look around your classroom. What states of matter do you see most? Name some solids in your classroom. A solid has a fixed shape and volume. The particles of a solid are packed tightly together.

You know all matter is made up of small particles. In most solids, the tightly-packed particles form a pattern. The pattern of particles repeats itself many times to form the solid. The patterns of particles packed together in a repeating order are called **crystals** (KRIHS tulz). The crystals for each kind of solid always have the same pattern or design. For example, all crystals of table salt have the same shape. Their shape is like a cubic box.

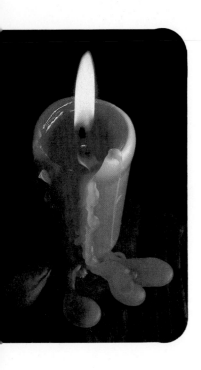

Solids are made of crystals. Solids have closely-spaced particles. The particles of solids are held together by an attraction. The attraction is strong in some solids. It is not so strong in other solids. The strength of the attraction affects how easily solids change to liquids. Solids with particles having a strong attraction are hard to change to liquids. Solids with particles having less of an attraction change to liquids more easily.

Some materials are not made of crystals. Glass, candle wax, and some plastics are examples of these materials. If pressure is applied to some of these materials, their shape will change. Think about a stick of butter. It seems to have a shape like a solid. Yet, its shape can be changed easily when you touch it. Materials which do not have crystals change to liquids slowly over a wide temperature range.

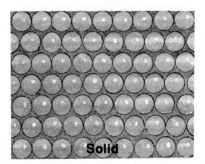

Solid

Solids Change State

When you heat a solid to a certain temperature, it melts. The temperature at which a solid becomes a liquid is called its **melting point.** Each solid made from crystals has its own melting point. For example, ice melts at 0°C.

Suppose you compare two solids, ice and metal. Ice melts from the heat of your hand. The metal in a house key will not melt when you hold it. The key must be heated to a very high temperature before it will melt. Both the ice cube and the metal key are solids. Both are made of particles that are packed tightly together. The particles have a strong attraction among them. In which solid is the attraction among particles stronger?

The particles in a liquid move faster than the particles in the solid state of the same material. Heating matter causes the particles to move faster. The more heat, the faster the particles move. They move farther apart, and the attraction among the particles is weakened. The crystal pattern breaks at the melting point. When the crystal pattern of the solid is gone throughout the solid, the solid has melted. The movement of particles is a property change you cannot see directly.

Liquid Matter

How is a liquid like a solid? What shape does the liquid in this container have? How can you change its shape? The particles of the same substance in a liquid state move faster than in a solid state. Therefore, their attraction for each other is less. Most liquid particles are not packed as tightly together as the particles in a solid. They tumble over and around each other. The particles in a liquid allow the liquid to flow when poured from one container to another. How are liquids different from solids?

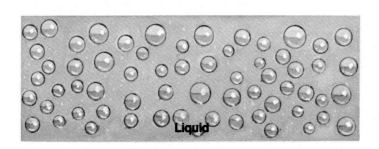
Liquid

Liquids Change State

A liquid can also change states. It can change to a solid or to a gas. Liquid water changes to a gas when heat energy is added.

The temperature at which a liquid has gained enough heat energy to change to a gas is the **boiling point** of the liquid. When a pan of water is fully boiling, where do you see the gas bubbles? Boiling occurs throughout the liquid. The boiling points of some materials are shown in the chart below. Which of these materials are gases at room temperature?

Boiling Points			
Substance	Boiling Point(°C)	Substance	Boiling Point (°C)
Bromine	59	Oxygen	-183
Mercury	357	Silver	2000
Nitrogen	−196	Lead	1740

Activity

What Is the Boiling Point of Water?

What to use:

hot plate	thermometer	watch or clock
one small pot	wooden ruler	hot pad glove
water	rubber band	pencil and paper

What to do:

1. Fill the pan ⅓ full of cold water.

2. Set it on the hot plate. **Do not** turn on the hot plate now.

3. Copy the chart shown below.

4. Attach the thermometer to a wooden ruler as shown. Adjust the thermometer so it stays about 3 cm above the bottom of the pan. **Do not allow the thermometer to touch the sides or bottom of the pan.**

5. Have your teacher turn on the hot plate to medium. CAUTION: Have your teacher use a hot pad glove to hold the thermometer.

6. Record the water temperature after each minute. Do this until the water has boiled for 5 minutes. Note the time when the water begins to boil.

Finding the Boiling Point of Water	
Time in Minutes	Water Temperature (°C)
1	
2	
3	
4	
5	
6	

What did you learn?

1. What happens to the temperature from minute to minute?

2. How long did it take the water to boil?

3. What is the boiling point temperature of water?

Using what you learned:

1. Make a graph with the information on your chart. How does the time increase compare to the temperature increase?

2. Where does the energy come from to boil the water?

The change of a liquid to a gas is called **evaporation** (ih vap uh RAY shun). Evaporation occurs when particles of a liquid escape from the surface of the liquid. It may take many hours or days for a rain puddle to change completely to water vapor in the air. The change takes place more quickly when more heat energy is added. On what kind of day would the evaporation of a rain puddle be the fastest?

Making Sure

1. What happens when a liquid changes to a gas?
2. What happens when a solid changes to a liquid?

Activity

What Affects the Rate of Evaporation?

What to use:
3 containers - different shapes and sizes
metric measuring cup
electric fan
water
pencil and paper

What to do:

1. Using the measuring cup, fill the three containers with exactly the same amount of water.

2. Predict and record from which container evaporation will occur the fastest.

3. Place the three containers in the same spot in your classroom.

4. You may wish to use a small fan during part of the day to increase the rate of evaporation.

5. Observe the water in the containers each day for 1 week. Make a record of your observations.

6. Compare your results with other classmates.

What did you learn?

1. From which container did the water evaporate fastest? Why do you think evaporation occurred fastest in that container?

2. How did your prediction compare with your experiment results?

3. How do your findings compare with others?

Using what you learned:

1. Why is it important to use the same amount of water in each container?

2. What could you do differently to improve your experiment?

3. In what kind of container should you keep flowers and water so the water will not evaporate easily?

Gas Matter

A gas has no fixed shape or volume. A gas takes the shape and becomes the volume of whatever container it fills. Heat energy makes the particles in a gas move fast. They move very far apart. The particles have very little attraction for one another. The gas fills its container completely. What are some common gases that are a part of your daily life?

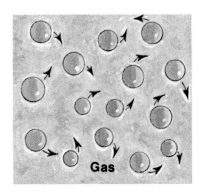

Gas

Activity

How Can We Use Gas Pressure?

What to use:

plastic bag   2 or 3 books   pencil and paper

What to do:

1. Place one book on top of the plastic bag as shown.

2. Blow air into the opening of the bag. Observe what happens.

3. Let the air out of the bag. Add several books, one at a time. Try to lift them by blowing air into the bag.

What did you learn?

1. What happened to the first book?
2. What happened as you added more books?

Using what you learned:

1. How does this experiment show that a gas applies pressure?
2. What would happen if there were holes in the plastic bag? Test your idea.
3. An air jack is a device to lift automobiles. How do you think it works?

Gases Change State

Gases also change state. Gases change to liquids. When enough heat energy is lost, a gas changes to a liquid by **condensation** (kahn den SAY shun). The particles move more slowly as the gas cools. The more heat energy the gas loses, the slower the gas particles move. They move closer together. The attraction between the gas particles increases. At a certain temperature, the gas particles move together to become a liquid again. We say that condensation has taken place.

You may have noticed dew on the grass on a summer morning. The dew comes from water vapor in the air when condensation occurs. The warmer air comes in contact with the cooler grass. The temperature of the air touching the grass is lowered. The water vapor in the air changes to a liquid.

When a liquid changes to a solid, it loses heat energy. A liquid loses heat energy when it cools. The particles of the liquid move more slowly as heat energy is lost. Particles move closer together. The attraction between them gets stronger as they get closer and closer. When the particles get very close, the attraction becomes great enough to hold them together in a fixed pattern. The liquid becomes a solid. Think about water when it changes from a liquid to a solid. What do you call the change of liquid water to ice?

The temperature at which a liquid becomes a solid is called its **freezing point.** Each liquid has a different freezing point. The chart below shows the freezing points of some materials. Are these materials solids or liquids at normal room temperature? (HINT: Room temperature is 20°C.)

Freezing Points	
Substance	Freezing Points (°C)
Water	0
Lead	328
Sugar	186
Mercury	−39
Iron	1535
Silver	962
Gold	1064

State Changes and Energy

Heat energy is part of all state changes. It is absorbed or given off in these changes. Think about the change of ice to water. What happens to the heat energy? If you wave your wet hands in the air, how do your hands feel? Water is evaporating from your hands. What happens to the heat energy of your hands? Why is it good that you sweat more on a hot day than on a cool day?

Each state of a substance has different amounts of heat energy. Which state has the most heat energy? The more heat energy matter has, the faster the particles move. The attraction between particles becomes less. Which state of matter has the least heat energy?

▬▬Chapter Review▬

Summary

- Matter can exist in three states.
- Solids have a fixed shape and volume.
- In solids, the tightly-packed particles form a pattern called a crystal.
- Liquids have a fixed volume but take the shape of their containers.
- Gases have no shape or volume of their own but fill and take the shape and volume of their containers.
- Matter can be changed from one state to another.
- Heat energy is absorbed or given off in all state changes.

Science Words

crystals	boiling point	condensation
melting point	evaporation	freezing point

Questions

1. If you see crystals, what state of matter are you observing?
2. How are solids different from liquids?
3. How are liquids different from gases?
4. How do the particles of matter act when changing from a solid to a liquid?
5. What causes the particles of matter to act differently and change from one state to another?
6. What state changes occur when heat energy is lost?
7. The freezing point occurs between what two states of matter?
8. The melting point occurs between what two states of matter?
9. Why do you feel cold after swimming on a warm day?
10. How are evaporation and boiling different?

 Self Checks

Answer these Self Checks on a sheet of paper.

1. Draw a model of the particles of a solid, a liquid, and a gas.
2. Why is weight an important property of matter?
3. When liquid is poured into a container, what property of liquid is shown?
4. Study the pictures below.
   (a) Which pictures show melting, evaporating, freezing, or condensing?
   (b) In which pictures is energy being absorbed?
   (c) In which pictures is energy being given off?

a

b

c

d

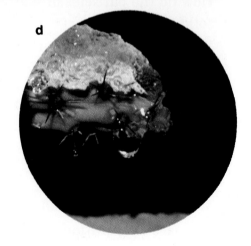

💡 Idea Corner
More Fun with Science

1. Design each of these words in a way that shows what each means: force, motion, evaporate, solid, liquid, gas.
   Example: melt

2. Find out what elements and compounds are mined in your state. Locate the mines on a map and report to your class.

3. Make a list of six towns or cities that are located at different elevations. For example, locate two on seashores, two in mountains, and two on the Great Plains. Write a letter to a fifth grade class in each one. Ask them to find the boiling point of water and send it to you. Compare the boiling points and elevations.

Reading for Fun

Einstein Anderson, Science Sleuth by Seymour Simon, Viking Press: New York, © 1980.
   Read how the hero uses scientific principles to solve mysteries.

How Did We Find Out About Atoms? by Isaac Asimov, Walker and Company: New York, © 1976.
   Find out how scientists discovered atoms.

Bet You Can't: Scientific Impossibilities to Fool You by Vicki Cobb and Kathy Darling, Avon Books: New York, © 1983.
   Learn the natural causes at work behind these "tricks."

Unit 3

Weather Patterns and Climate

Chapter One
Air Affects Weather

Who needs to know about weather? What factors affect the weather? How would you describe the weather in the picture?

How did you decide what to wear to school today? What will you do after school today? Often what you wear and what you do depend on the weather. A sudden change in weather may change your plans. Everyone is affected by the weather. Weather is important to everyone.

Weather is the condition of the air around us. The air is always changing. It becomes warmer or colder. The wind changes speed and direction. Air can be moist or dry. All of these factors are part of weather. Learning about air will help you understand weather.

The Earth's Atmosphere

A blanket of air called the **atmosphere** (AT muh sfihr) surrounds the Earth. The atmosphere is a mixture of gases in several layers. It extends from the Earth's surface to about 800 km above the Earth. You have to run around a football field about 3000 times to go that far!

The layer of the atmosphere closest to the Earth's surface is called the **troposphere** (TROHP uh sfihr). The troposphere contains water and mostly the gases nitrogen and oxygen. Most weather occurs in the troposphere. Troposphere conditions change quickly.

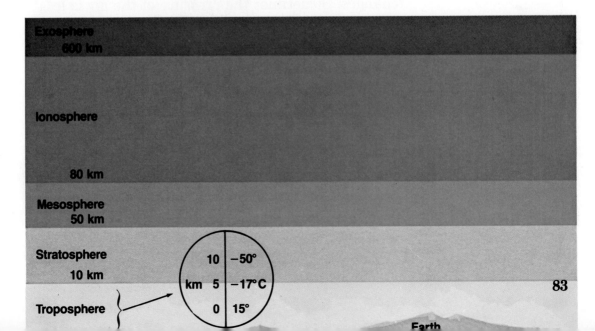

Exosphere
600 km

Ionosphere

80 km

Mesosphere
50 km

Stratosphere
10 km

km	
10	−50°
5	−17°C
0	15°

Troposphere

Earth

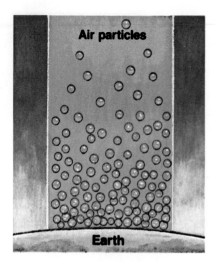

Air particles

Earth

The other layers of the atmosphere change very little. Because people live in the troposphere, it is important to understand how the air changes here.

Study the diagram of the Earth's atmosphere on page 83. Look carefully at the troposphere. What is the temperature at the surface of the Earth? Find the temperature of the air at 3 km, 5 km, and 10 km above the Earth's surface. What happens to the temperature higher in the troposphere?

Look at the air particles in the drawing of the atmosphere. Compare the number of air particles near the Earth's surface with the number of air particles higher in the atmosphere. Why do you think there are more particles near the Earth's surface?

Gravity causes a ball to fall to the Earth. Gravity also pulls the atmosphere to the Earth's surface. Gravity causes the gases to be pressed down on the Earth's surface. The pressing down of the air on the Earth's surface is called **air pressure.**

Air Pressure

Air pressure is a property of air that often changes. Sometimes the pressure of the air is less than at other times. An area of low pressure is called a low on a weather map. An area of high pressure is called a high on a weather map.

Air pressure is measured with a **barometer** (buh RAHM ut ur). Any changes in air pressure are shown by this instrument. A falling air pressure reading on the barometer is often a sign of bad weather. A rising barometer reading means high pressure or a high is coming. A high often means good weather. A steady barometer reading means the weather will remain the same.

Here is a type of barometer. What air pressure does it show? Where have you seen barometers like this one?

Making Sure

1. In what layer of the atmosphere does most weather take place?
2. Why does the atmosphere have air pressure?

Air Temperature

Temperature is another property of air that changes. Air temperature is measured with an instrument called a thermometer. Notice that the chart shows both the time of the day and the temperature. Describe what happens to the temperature at different times of the day. Why are there changes?

Day Temperatures Birmingham, AL July 20	
Time	Temp. (°C)
7:00 a.m.	21
9:00 a.m.	25
11:00 a.m.	29
1:00 p.m.	32
3:00 p.m.	33
5:00 p.m.	31
7:00 p.m.	28

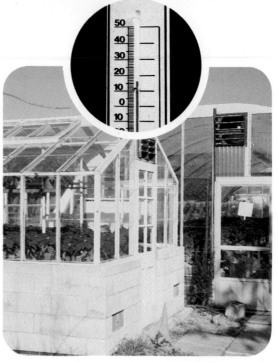

What causes air temperature to become warm? Think of the Earth and its atmosphere as a greenhouse. Air in a greenhouse is warmed by the sun. Energy from the sun also warms the Earth's atmosphere. Both the atmosphere and the greenhouse glass let in energy from the sun. Energy from the sun is absorbed by the Earth's surface and surfaces in the greenhouse. This energy is changed to heat energy. Most of the heat energy cannot escape from the Earth's atmosphere or the greenhouse glass. Trapped heat energy warms the air.

Activity

How Do Surfaces Affect Air Temperature?

What to use:

stick   clock or watch
tape   pencil and paper
thermometer

What to do:

1. Select at least four different locations around your school building. Choose sunny places with different kinds of surfaces—grass, soil, hardtop driveway, gravel driveway, and so on.

2. Make a chart like the one below. Fill in the chart now to predict what the air temperatures will be.

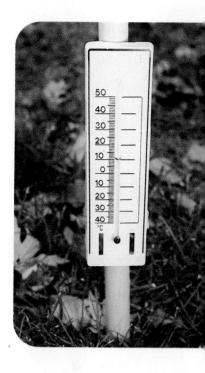

Surface Temperatures			
Location	Surface	Prediction of Air Temperature (°C)	Actual Air Temperature (°C)
1.			
2.			
3.			
4.			

3. Tape the thermometer to the stick so that the thermometer bulb is 10 cm above the ground.

4. Go to each location and measure the air temperature. Stand the stick straight up and hold it for 2 minutes or long enough for the liquid in the thermometer to stop moving. After 2 minutes, read the thermometer. Record the temperature on your chart.

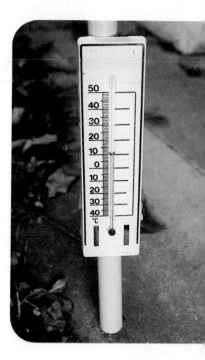

What did you learn?

1. What were the lowest and highest temperatures?
2. What kind of surface had the lowest reading?
3. What kind of surface had the highest reading?
4. How do your predictions compare with the actual readings?

Using what you learned:

1. What surface would warm your cold drink fastest?
2. On what surface would you rather walk barefoot on a hot sunny day? Why?

One kind of surface may absorb more of the sun's energy than another. Some surfaces take longer to become warm than other surfaces. For example, water takes a longer time to warm than land. The unequal heating of the Earth's surface causes air movement.

Air Movement

Another property of air is movement. The sideways movement of air is called wind. Gentle winds can be very pleasant. Strong winds can cause much damage. What activities do you do that need wind? How do people use wind to do work?

Wind moves from areas of higher air pressure to areas of lower air pressure. Study the weather map on this page. The arrows show the way wind moves out of highs and into lows. How does air move around highs? How does air move around lows?

Wind is named for the direction from which it comes. A north wind blows from north to south. A west wind blows from west to east. Suppose you see the wind blowing leaves to the northeast. What is the name of the wind?

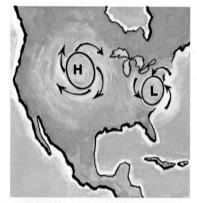

A wind vane shows which way the wind blows. It points to the direction from which the wind is blowing. There are many kinds of wind vanes. Look at this one. From which direction is the wind blowing? What would you call the wind?

Flags also show wind direction. How are they different from wind vanes? Smoke can also show wind direction. Is smoke more like a wind vane or a flag? Why? What else have you seen that shows wind direction?

Wind changes speed as well as direction. Wind speed is measured by an instrument called an **anemometer** (an uh MAHM ut ur). An anemometer has cups that turn from the wind. The stronger the wind blows, the faster the cups turn. The gauge of an anemometer is marked in meters per second. What is the wind speed shown by the anemometer here?

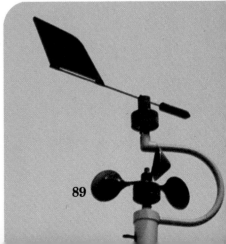

Activity

How Do Buildings Affect Wind Direction?

What to use:

feather vane   pencil and paper

What to do:

1. Draw a map of your schoolyard.

2. Choose and mark on your map six different stations around the outside of the school building. Each station should be about one meter from the building walls.

3. Choose a windy day. Notice your school flag or the tree branches to determine the wind direction.

4. Use the feather vane provided by your teacher. Place it on the ground at each station. Record the wind direction at each station on your map. Draw arrows to show wind direction.

What did you learn?

1. What was the general wind direction during the activity?

2. How did the wind direction differ at each station?

3. At which station was the feather vane most affected?

4. At which station was the feather vane least affected?

5. How does the air move around buildings?

Using what you learned:

1. How does the wind direction near buildings differ from the wind direction in an open area?

2. How does the air move around the many buildings in a city?

Before the anemometer was invented, people used other ways to find wind speed. In 1805, a man named Beaufort (BOH furt) made a scale to judge wind speed. The scale is called the Beaufort scale. The **Beaufort scale** is a scale that shows numbers for wind speed. Notice the Beaufort scale numbers on the chart.

Beaufort Number	Symbol	Land Description	Wind Speed km/h	U.S. Weather Term
0	◎	Calm; smoke rises straight up.	Less than 1	Calm
1		Smoke drifts. Wind vanes do not move.	1 – 5	
2		Wind felt on face. Wind vanes move. Leaves rustle.	6 – 11	Light breeze
3		Leaves and twigs move. Flags wave slightly.	12 – 19	Gentle breeze
4		Dust and bits of paper blow about. Small branches move.	20 – 28	Moderate breeze
5		Small trees sway. White waves on lakes and ponds.	29 – 38	
6		Large branches move. Umbrellas hard to use.	39 – 49	Strong breeze
7		Whole trees sway. Difficult to walk against wind.	50 – 61	
8		Twigs break off trees.	62 – 74	
9		Small damage to buildings. Shingles blown off roof.	75 – 88	
10		Trees uprooted. Considerable damage to buildings.	89 – 102	Gale
11		Widespread damage.	103 – 117	Storm
12-17		Rarely experienced. Reaching hurricane speeds.	More than 117	Hurricane

Cirrus clouds

Cumulus clouds

Air Moisture

Another property of air is moisture. Moisture in the air can be in the form of a gas, a liquid, or a solid. One type of air moisture is a gas called water vapor. You cannot see water vapor.

The amount of water vapor in the air is called **humidity** (hyew MIHD ut ee). When the air contains lots of water vapor, the humidity is high. Air with little vapor has low humidity. Air temperature affects the humidity. Warm air holds more water vapor. Cold air cannot hold as much. As air becomes colder, it holds less and less water vapor. **Relative humidity** tells the comparison of water vapor and air temperature. Relative humidity of 100% means the air is holding all the water vapor it can at that temperature. What is 50% relative humidity?

When warm air rises, it becomes cooler. At cooler temperatures, water vapor condenses to form clouds. Unlike water vapor, clouds are forms of moisture you can see.

Cirrus (SIHR us) **clouds** are thin, white clouds with featherlike edges. They form at high levels in the troposphere and are made of ice crystals. Cirrus clouds usually mean good weather.

Cumulus (KYEW myuh lus) **clouds** are large, puffy clouds. They are often seen in good weather, too. They are much thicker and lower in the sky than cirrus clouds. Their shapes change all the time.

Stratus clouds

Fog

Cumulus clouds are often very white with gray centers. Heavy dark cumulus clouds are storm clouds. They may produce rain or snow showers and thunderstorms.

Stratus clouds look like thick layers that form a blanket over the land. Little sunlight can shine through stratus layers. The layers appear gray or dark during the day. Stratus clouds may produce rain or snow. Suppose a thick layer of stratus clouds moved in over your area. How could you tell whether it may rain or snow?

One special type of stratus cloud is fog. Fog is a stratus cloud close to the ground. What is it like outdoors when there is fog? If you have walked through fog, you have walked through a cloud. Most fogs are stratus clouds made of very tiny water drops. Some fog in cold areas is made of ice crystals.

When the water drops that form clouds come together, they form larger drops. The larger drops come together to form even larger drops. When the drops are large and heavy enough, they fall to the Earth as rain. Rain is precipitation (prih sihp uh TAY shun). **Precipitation** is water returning to the Earth's surface from the atmosphere. You can see and feel precipitation. Water drops or ice crystals in the clouds change into precipitation if they become large enough to fall. Falling water drops are called rain or drizzle. What other forms of precipitation can you name?

People and Science

Clearing the Way!

In areas of cold and snowy climates, workers must remove the snow and ice from roads. Snowplows are used to remove the snow. Driving a snowplow is a dangerous but necessary job.

The snowplow driver uses several kinds of snowplows to clear the road. A V-shaped or straightedge blade attaches to the front of large trucks to push the snow aside. Plows with round-shaped blades are used in areas where the snow is very deep. The blades pull the snow into the front of the truck. Then the snow goes into a huge fan where it is shot up onto the side of the road. Some snowplow drivers also spread sand, salt, other chemicals, or cinders on the road from the rear of their trucks. These materials help make the road less slippery.

Snowdrifts can block roads which have already been cleared if it is windy. Thin picket snow fences are placed along the side of the road to help the snowplow operator. These fences keep the snow from blowing onto the highways.

Snowplow drivers must pay careful attention to the weather forecasts. Whenever a storm hits, the driver must be ready to plow. The roads may be dangerous and the weather can be very unpleasant, but the roads must be cleared!

Chapter Review

Summary

- Weather is the condition of the air around us.
- Air pressure, temperature, movement, and moisture are parts of the weather.
- A barometer, a thermometer, a wind vane, and an anemometer are used to measure different properties of air.
- Air pressure changes usually mean weather changes.
- Humidity is moisture in the air you cannot see.
- Relative humidity indicates how much moisture is in the air at a certain temperature.
- Cirrus, cumulus, and stratus are three types of clouds.
- Precipitation is water returning to the Earth's surface.

Science Words

atmosphere	anemometer	cirrus clouds
troposphere	Beaufort scale	cumulus clouds
air pressure	humidity	stratus clouds
barometer	relative humidity	precipitation

Questions

1. Name four properties of the troposphere.
2. What instruments are used to measure air properties?
3. Which property does each instrument measure?
4. Would a barometer more likely read high or low on a very cloudy day?
5. If wind is coming out of the northwest, in which direction will the wind vane point?
6. What is the difference between humidity and relative humidity?
7. What does 76% relative humidity mean?
8. Name and describe three types of clouds.

Chapter Two
Weather Affects Climate

How would you describe the weather in this picture? What is the season of the year? How does the weather change as the seasons change?

Today it may be sunny and warm. What will the weather be tomorrow? You can find out by listening to a weather report on the radio or TV.

Predicting the Weather

The weather report includes a forecast. A **forecast** is a prediction of what the weather will be. A forecast is made from a careful study of air pressure, temperature, wind, and moisture. The changes in the conditions of the air are observed and measured to make a forecast.

Meteorologists (meet ee uh RAHL uh justs) are scientists who study the weather. They collect weather information or data from many places. Meteorologists use this data to make weather maps. Weather satellites orbit the Earth and send back pictures of cloud patterns. Meteorologists use weather maps and satellite pictures to predict weather changes.

Activity

How Do You Read a Weather Map?

What to use:

weather map   station model
symbol chart   pencil and paper

Weather Map

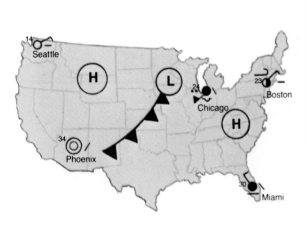

Symbol Chart				
Sky Conditions	○ Clear	◔ Quarter covered	◑ Half covered	● Completely covered
Wind Speed and Direction	○ 0 calm	12-19 km/h	29-38 km/h	75-88 km/h
Cloud Type	Cirrus	Thick Alto-stratus	Strato-cumulus	Stratus
Precipitation	≡ Fog	✳ ✳ Snow	● ● Rain	Thunder-storm
Fronts and Pressure Systems	(H) or High (L) or Low	Cold front		Warm front
Barometer	Rising	Steady		Falling

What to do:

Study the weather map, symbol chart, and station model.

Station Model

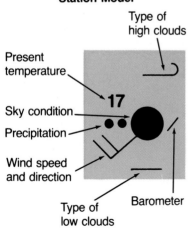

Type of high clouds

Present temperature

17

Sky condition

Precipitation

Wind speed and direction

Type of low clouds

Barometer

What did you learn?

1. What do the symbols ✳ ✳, ◑ , and ⌄ mean?
2. Use the weather map and station model to answer these questions.
   (a) What is the wind direction and speed in Boston?
   (b) In Miami, approximately how much of the sky is covered by clouds? What type of clouds are they?
   (c) What is the air temperature in Phoenix?
   (d) Is the barometer rising, falling, or steady at Boston?

98

(e) What data is given about precipitation at Chicago?

3. Houston reports 21°, quarter sky covering, fog, steady barometer, and calm. Make a station model using this data.

Using what you learned:

1. Why do you think meteorologists use symbols?
2. What changes would you expect in Chicago weather data after the cold front moves east?

The Key to Forecasts

Large bodies of air moving across land and water are called **air masses.** The temperature and humidity are about the same throughout an air mass. In the United States, most air masses move from west to east. Meteorologists observe these air masses carefully. They know that a new air mass moving into an area often brings weather changes. By studying the new air mass, they can forecast weather changes.

Meteorologists find out where air masses are formed to help them forecast the weather. Each air mass has properties like the surface over which it forms. If an air mass forms over water, it will become very moist or humid. An air mass that forms over land is usually dry. An air mass coming from a cold area has low temperatures. An air mass moving from a warm or hot area has high temperatures.

As an air mass moves into an area, air temperature and amount of moisture change. If a dry, cold air mass moved into your area in summer, you would have cool, dry weather and clear skies. In winter, the air mass would bring cold and dry weather with clear skies. What might a warm, moist air mass in summer mean?

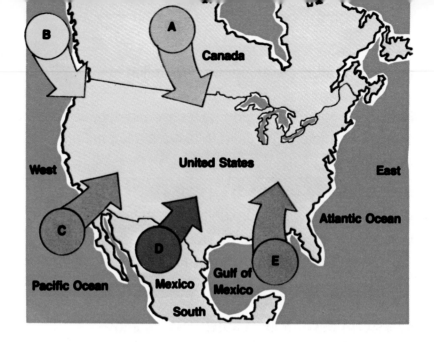

This map shows where air masses come from that affect the weather in the United States. The arrows show the direction these air masses often move. Notice the area where each forms. Describe the temperature and moisture conditions of each. What kind of weather would each bring in winter?

When Air Masses Meet

Moving air masses often come in contact with each other. The place where two air masses meet is called a **front.** A warm front forms when a warm air mass moves into a cold air mass. A cold front forms when a cold air mass pushes into a warm air mass.

Meteorologists carefully watch fronts to forecast the weather. Sometimes, warm air is lifted rapidly by the cold air in a cold front. The lifting movement of warm air may cause storms with heavy rain

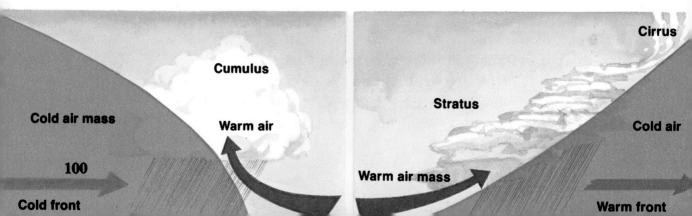

showers. Cold fronts usually pass quickly. They generally move faster than warm fronts.

Warm air slides over cold air along a warm front. Warm fronts take longer to pass through an area. Steady rains or snow may occur along warm fronts. What kinds of clouds do you expect to form along warm fronts? The locations of fronts are shown on weather maps with symbols.

Storms

If warm air along fronts is lifted upward, a thunderstorm may occur. **Thunderstorms** are strong, local storms with lightning, thunder, and sometimes hail. Thunderstorms may form when warm moist air is forced up by a front. Also, thunderstorms form when moist air rises rapidly because it is strongly heated by the sun.

During a severe thunderstorm, tornadoes (tor NAYD ohz) may occur. **Tornadoes** are strong windstorms that have clouds shaped like funnels. Even though tornadoes are small compared to other storms, they are very strong and can cause much damage. High winds can uproot trees, tear apart buildings, and lift cars.

Weather bulletins and sirens are used to warn people of tornadoes. What should you do when you hear a tornado warning? Tornadoes occur most often in spring and early summer. They often form in late afternoon or early evening. How common are tornadoes where you live?

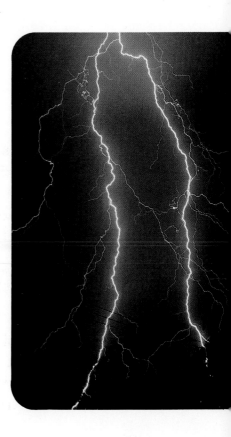

The Winter Storm

Dear Carla,

There is no school today. I am home from school because of large snow drifts and cold temperatures. I barely made it home from school when the blizzard started. It was very scary as we rode the bus in those winds. It has lasted almost two days. I heard later the winds were up to seventy kilometers per hour. Some tree branches were blowing past the window. At times, all I could see was a white cloud of snow around the bus. The usual twenty minute drive from school took an hour.

Some of the snow is piling up around our house in drifts. These drifts are about two meters high. Outside our kitchen door one snowdrift is even higher.

There is no electricity to run the water pump, so we have no water. We melt the snow from outside for drinking. The outside temperature has dropped to -20°C. Heat from a small wood burning stove in the living room keeps us warm. We use gas for cooking.

It is an uneasy feeling being snowed in and not being able to go anywhere. We don't know when we will be able to dig out. The windows are completely covered with snow. When I look out, all I see is a thick cloud of hazy white. The wind is howling and screaming, letting up a little at times.

I hope your weather is better than ours. Write soon.

Your friend,
Cheryl

Hurricanes are storms with strong winds and heavy rains. Unlike other storms, hurricanes occur over a large area and last a long time. If you were a meteorologist, you would look for a hurricane forming in a very low pressure area over warm, tropical oceans. Most hurricanes occur in late summer and early fall.

Hurricanes begin over the ocean, but they can move to the shore. At the shore, they cause huge waves which do much damage to land. The swirling winds are about half the speed of the fastest tornadoes. The high winds can destroy trees and buildings. Water damage from the heavy rains and floods can occur hundreds of kilometers from the hurricane's center, or eye. Weather forecasts warn people of the possible flooding and wind damage from hurricanes. Most hurricanes move hundreds of kilometers from where they began. The results of the storm may be seen for weeks and months.

Weather Year After Year

Suppose you wanted to take a trip to Alaska in winter. What kind of clothes would you take on the trip? Why is it important to have the right clothes?

You would need to know what kind of weather to expect. You want to know about the climate (KLI mut). **Climate** is the average weather of an area for many years.

The weather of an area changes from day to day. However, the climate of an area stays the same year after year. If your trip is to Hawaii in winter, you can expect the weather to be warm. Hawaii has been warm and sunny for many winters.

What Makes a Climate?

Meteorologists observe some factors of the weather to find the climate of an area. Temperature throughout the year is an important factor of climate. The high and low temperatures for each day are recorded. Then the average or middle temperature is found. The average temperature for a day is called the **daily mean.** You can find the daily mean for your area. Find the highest and lowest temperatures for the day. Add them together. Divide your answer by two. Your answer is the daily mean temperature for that day. How could you find the average temperature for a week or a month? Average daily mean temperatures during a certain season are different for different climates. In winter, how do the average daily mean temperatures in Florida compare with those in Montana?

Temperature is not the only factor of climate. The precipitation for each year is also an important part of climate. A rain gauge is used to collect and measure rain, snow, and sleet. Precipitation is often measured in centimeters in the rain gauge. Snow and sleet must be melted before they can be measured. What is the amount of precipitation in this rain gauge?

The form of precipitation and the season of the year are also important parts of climate. A snowy, cold climate means there is much precipitation during a cold winter. What would a dry, warm climate in winter mean?

In what part of the year does your area receive the most precipitation? What form of precipitation is it? Which place in the pictures is most like your climate? Which has the wettest climate? Which shows the driest climate? Which shows the warmest climate?

The same air masses that determine weather also affect climate. Suppose warm moist air moves over

an area most of the year. What kind of climate would you find there? Usually places with moist climates are found near large bodies of water. Gila Bend, Arizona, has a hot, dry, sunny climate. What kind of air mass can usually be found there in the summer?

Making Sure

1. Weather forecasts are made from a careful study of weather factors. What are these factors?
2. How do air masses affect the weather of an area?

Why Do Climates Differ?

To compare climates, you must compare temperature and precipitation. Why are some places very warm while others are very cold? Why are some areas very wet while others are very dry?

The way the sun's rays strike the Earth has a lot to do with climate. The sun's rays do not strike each part of the Earth in the same way. Some parts of the Earth receive direct rays of the sun. Direct rays occur when the sun is straight overhead in the sky. Other parts of the Earth never receive direct rays. Which climate factor do you think is changed most by the way the sun's rays hit the Earth?

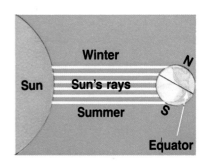

107

Activity

Why Are the Sun's Rays Indirect Over Part of the Earth?

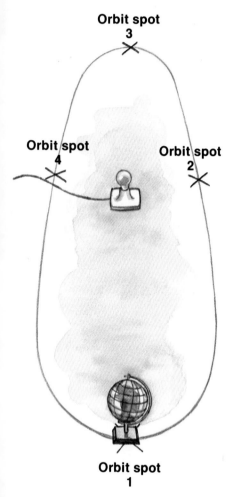

Orbit spot 3

Orbit spot 4

Orbit spot 2

Orbit spot 1

What to use:

globe   chalk or masking tape
light bulb   pencil and paper

What to do:

1. Draw the Earth's orbit on the floor with chalk or masking tape. (Use an area of about 2 m by 3 m.) Mark a spot at each ¼ part of the orbit as shown.

2. Place the light bulb in the middle of the orbit and turn it on. Darken the room.

3. Place the globe on each orbit spot. (Make sure the rod through the center of the globe points in the same direction at each of the four marked orbit spots.) Observe what parts of the globe are light and what parts are dark in each orbit spot.

What did you learn?

1. Where is most of the light on the globe in the first orbit spot?
2. Where is most of the light on the globe in the second orbit spot?
3. Where is most of the light in the third and fourth orbit spots?
4. Where does the light hit the globe most directly?

Using what you learned:

1. What orbit spot would the Earth be in during each of your seasons?
2. What caused the sun's direct rays to change?

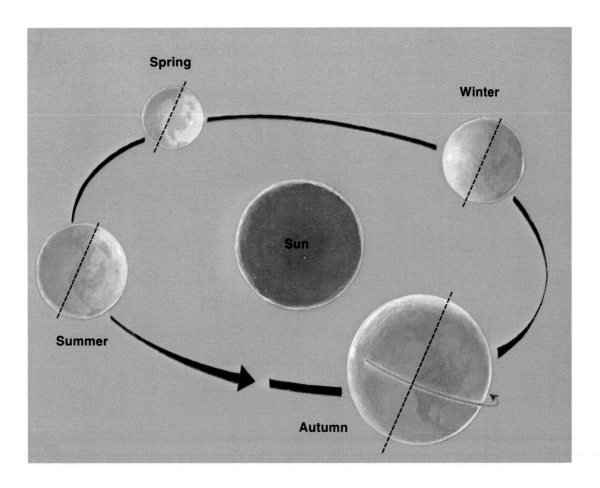

Spring

Winter

Summer

Sun

Autumn

You may notice there is a rod through the center of a globe. The rod of a globe is like the imaginary rod through the center of the Earth. The imaginary rod is called an axis (AK sus). The Earth's axis is tipped or tilted like it is on the globe. The direction of the tilt does not change as the Earth moves in its orbit around the sun. Direct rays from the sun strike south or north of the equator because of the tilt of the axis. The tilt of the Earth and the orbit are what cause the seasons.

During each season, you are aware of the sun's heat energy. You feel much warmer in summer than you feel in winter. The sun's rays are more direct or less slanted in summer. Less direct rays cause heat energy to be spread out over a larger area. Therefore, you feel cooler during the winter season.

Some parts of the world have four seasons each year. These places never receive direct rays from the sun. Yet, the rays are more direct in summer than in winter. How does the direction of the sun's rays change the temperature of the air in summer? How does the direction of the sun's rays change the temperature of the air in winter?

Activity

How Do the Direct Rays of the Sun Heat the Earth?

What to use:

2 thermometers   pencil and paper
2 boxes of sand

What to do:

1. Be sure both thermometers are at the same temperature. Record the temperatures. Put a thermometer in each box of sand.

2. Place both boxes in the sun. Place one box so it is lying flat. Lean the second box up against some books as shown.

3. Wait 5 minutes. Record the temperature shown by each thermometer.

What did you learn?

1. Which box received the more direct rays of the sun?
2. Which box had the higher temperature?

Using what you learned:

1. How do the sun's rays strike your area in summer? How do they strike your area in winter? Why?
2. What kind of climate do you have? Why?

Chapter Review

Summary

- Meteorologists study air masses to make weather forecasts.
- Air masses have properties of the area over which they form.
- A front is where two different air masses come together.
- Temperature and precipitation are important factors of climate.
- Climates differ because of the way the sun's rays strike the Earth.
- The tilt of the axis and orbit of the Earth cause the change of seasons.

Science Words

forecast	front	hurricanes
meteorologists	thunderstorms	climate
air masses	tornadoes	daily mean

Questions

1. Why are air masses important to meteorologists?
2. If a moist, cold air mass were coming into your area in summer, what kind of weather would you expect?
3. How do warm and cold fronts change the weather?
4. What are local storms with thunder and lightning called?
5. What kind of storm is sometimes located along cold fronts?
6. What storms generally form over the ocean but can move to land causing much damage?
7. What is the difference between weather and climate?
8. Name the two factors which can change climate the most.
9. Why are the sun's rays indirect over part of the Earth?
10. What is the imaginary rod through the Earth's center called?

Self Checks

Answer these Self Checks on a sheet of paper.

1. In what part of the atmosphere does weather take place?

2. What climate factor is changed by the way the sun's rays hit the Earth?

3. Describe the difference between cumulus and stratus clouds.

4. How is the temperature of the air over a warm surface different from the temperature of the air over a cold surface?

5. Describe the characteristics of an air mass which forms over Mexico and Arizona.

6. How are warm and cold fronts alike? How are they different?

7. Describe the differences between tornadoes and hurricanes.

8. What properties of the air are measured by each of these instruments?

a

b

c

d

☀ Idea Corner
More Fun with Science

1. Gather pictures that show different climates. Use them to make a mobile.
2. Make a temperature map of the many surfaces and areas around the outside of your home.
3. Write a poem about climate conditions for each season of the year where you live.
4. Watch a TV weather program for one week. Observe the weather patterns and record the forecasts given. How accurate were the forecasts?
5. Set up your own weather station, constructing the equipment to measure air factors. Make a chart to record air temperature, wind speed and direction, cloud cover and type, and precipitation. Display your records in the classroom.
6. Cut out newspaper weather maps and put them on the bulletin board for a week. Watch the movements of fronts, temperature and pressure changes, and precipitation areas. Use the information to predict the weather each day.

Reading for Fun

Nature's Weather Forecasters by Helen R. Sattler, Thomas Nelson, Inc.: Nashville, © 1978.

Learn the scientific facts behind folk tales about the weather.

The Weather by Frank Dalton, Crane-Russak: New York, © 1977.

Learn about all kinds of weather and its effect on people.

What's Happening to Our Climate? by Malcolm E. Weiss, Julian Messner: New York, © 1978.

Explore reasons for changes in weather patterns.

Unit 4

The Human Body

Chapter One

Skin: The Body Covering

What is the outer covering of this animal? What is your body covering called? How does it protect you?

The covering of an object gives protection. The brick or siding on your school shields you and the furniture from rain, snow, sun, and wind. The walls shield the classrooms from the hot sun and cold air. What happens to a peeled orange after a few hours? What protects the inside of the orange?

Covering System

You also have a covering. It is called the body covering system. The **body covering system** is the skin, the hair, and the nails.

The outside covering of your body is **skin.** The skin is made of different tissues. It is the largest organ of your body since it covers so much area. Skin protects your body from germs, dirt, dryness, and harmful sun rays. Correct body temperature is partly controlled by the skin, too.

Human skin is very thin compared to an orange peel. Although the skin is thin, it has two parts. These parts are the epidermis (ep uh DUR mus) and the dermis (DUR mus). The **epidermis** is the outer or top skin layer you can see. "Epi" means upon or over. The epidermis is "upon the dermis." The **dermis** is the inner skin layer below the epidermis. You cannot see the dermis unless the epidermis has been injured. What do you think "dermis" means?

Epidermis

The epidermis is less than a millimeter thick. The outer part of the epidermis has a waterproof substance. This substance keeps water from soaking into your body. The waterproof substance also helps to prevent water from evaporating out of the body.

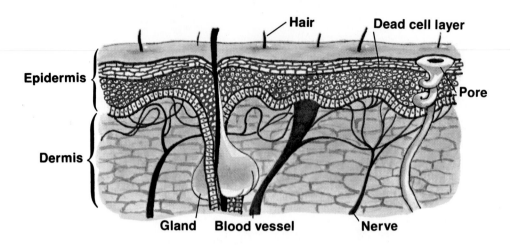

It is important that the body does not lose too much water. Body cells and tissues are made mostly of water. If the cells lose too much water, they will die. The waterproof substance of the epidermis also acts as a guard to keep dirt, germs, and chemicals from entering the body.

Cells at the bottom of the epidermis are alive. They make new skin cells. The new cells are pushed outward to replace the dead cells that rub off. Soon the live cells become the outer cells. These cells will protect you until they die and are rubbed off. Everytime you take a bath or shower, you wash off millions of dead cells. The white flakes of the dead cells from your scalp are called dandruff.

Dermis

The dermis is much thicker than the epidermis. It may be three or more millimeters thick. The dermis is made of living cells. Nerves and blood vessels are in this layer of skin. Blood supplies food and oxygen to the skin cells. The blood also takes away cell wastes.

The dermis contains hair roots and some glands. **Glands** are special groups of cells that produce and store substances. Some glands are oil glands. They release an oily liquid that keeps the skin soft and smooth.

The oil rises to the skin's surface through pores. **Pores** are small openings in the skin. The pores let the oil travel from the glands in the dermis to the skin's surface.

Other glands in the dermis are sweat glands. Sweat glands also have pores that open onto the surface of the skin. Sweat and cell wastes move from the glands through the pores to the surface of the skin. You see wet skin as a result of sweat. As the moisture from the sweat evaporates, the body cools.

The skin can cool the body in another way, too. When the body becomes too warm, the blood vessels in the dermis expand or get larger. More blood flows to the skin. The red skin is caused by expanded blood vessels and increased blood flow to the skin. As the blood flows to the skin, body heat in the blood leaves through the skin.

Making Sure

1. Name the two parts of the skin.
2. How does your skin protect you?

Activity

What Do Skin Cells Look Like?

What to use:

microscope	toothpicks
glass slides	dropper
coverslips	water
hand lens	pencil and paper

What to do:

1. Use a hand lens to observe the skin on the back of your hand.

2. Locate some dry skin on the back of your hand or around your fingernails. Rub some of the dry skin onto a glass slide.

3. Place a drop of water on the skin and carefully lower a coverslip into place.

4. Observe the skin cells under low power of the microscope.

5. Draw what you observe on a piece of paper.

What did you learn?

1. What did your skin look like in step 1?
2. What are the shapes of skin cells?
3. What else did you observe besides skin cells?

Using what you learned:

1. Why is a microscope needed to observe skin cells?
2. How does the size and shape of a skin cell protect you?
3. What layer of skin cells did you observe?

Skin Color

People have many different skin colors. The color of skin is caused by a pigment (PIHG munt). **Pigment** is a substance in the dermis that gives color to skin. Skin pigment is brown. A person with a small amount of pigment has lighter-colored skin. A person with a large amount of pigment has darker-colored skin. Freckles on the skin are areas where much pigment is close together.

Skin pigment shields body tissue from the harmful rays of the sun. Pigment protects the skin from sunburn. The more pigment you have, the more protection you have from the sun. How does the sun affect your skin?

Increasing your time in the sun can increase the pigment in your skin. The sun causes your skin to produce more pigment. The increase of pigment may show as freckles or as a tan. If you are going to be in the sun, it is important to control the time your skin is uncovered. A little sun each day can be healthy. The pigment will slowly build up in the skin and block the harmful rays. You will not get a sunburn. However, too much sun can burn your skin. To be safe, do not spend too much time in the sun.

Nails and Hair

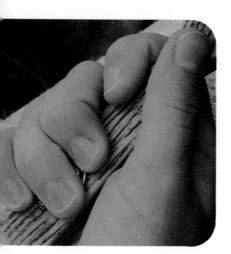

The body covering system has some special cells that form nails and hair. Nails protect the ends of your fingers and toes.

Nails are made of both living and dead cells. The base of each nail is in the dermis. New nail cells form in the dermis and push the dead cells out to the epidermis. Is the part of the nail you see alive or dead? Why does it not hurt to trim your nails? Why must nails be trimmed often?

Hair color can be white, black, or any color between white and black. Like skin color, hair color depends on the amount of pigment. The more pigment you have, the darker the hair. Pigment is

found in the hair roots. Some common hair colors are shades of blond and brown. As they grow older most people produce less pigment than when they were younger. Why do you think some people have white or gray hair?

Some people have curly or wavy hair. The amount of curl depends on the shape of the hairs. Curly hair is flat. The flatter the shape, the curlier the hair. Straight hair is round. Which kind do you have?

Care of the Body Covering System

How do you care for your skin, nails, and hair? The body covering system needs to be kept clean in order to be healthy and work well. You should bathe often to remove dirt and some of the oil which may clog pores. Clogged pores do not allow the body to remove wastes. If the pores are clogged, pimples may form. You can avoid some pimples by keeping your skin clean.

Nails and hair are made of protein (PROH teen). They need protein to grow. Cheese, peanut butter, eggs, meats, and fish are all good sources of protein. How much protein do you eat each day?

Proper exercise and rest are also necessary for healthy skin. Exercise causes blood to flow well through the dermis. Blood carries the needed minerals, vitamins, and proteins to the dermis for cell growth. Blood carries the waste products away from the skin cells, too. Sleep allows the body functions to slow down and is important for all body functions. Healthful food, sleep, exercise, and bathing are all necessary for a healthy body covering system.

People and Science

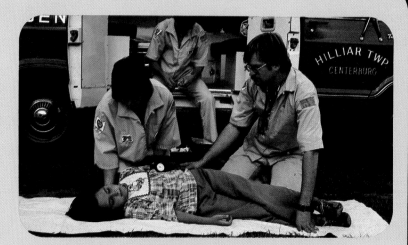

A Call for HELP!

What does the sound of a siren mean to you? When Joan Pendle and Tom Bennett hear a siren, they know that someone is answering a call for help. Joan and Tom are emergency paramedics (PER uh med iks) of the rescue squad. Paramedics are special members of the fire department. They know how to help people who are sick or hurt in emergencies.

Already today Joan and Tom have answered a call for help. A ten-year-old child had broken a leg. Joan and Tom checked the child for injuries. They measured the child's pulse, blood pressure, and breathing. They transported the child to the hospital in the rescue squad vehicle. The rescue squad is equipped with medicine and supplies for helping people. With a two-way radio, paramedics can talk with doctors at a nearby hospital. At the hospital, doctors and nurses will be ready to help.

When there are no calls for help, Joan and Tom have other work to do. They write reports and keep the rescue squad well-stocked.

Joan and Tom are eating lunch now. Suddenly they hear the emergency bell! A man is having a heart attack. In seconds, Joan and Tom are on their way. Paramedics must be quick. A few minutes delay may mean the difference between life and death for someone. Joan and Tom are always ready to help.

124

Chapter Review

Summary

- The body covering system includes the skin, hair, and nails.
- The epidermis is thin and consists mostly of dead cells.
- The dermis contains nerves and blood vessels.
- Skin glands are special cells that produce oils and sweat.
- Pores carry oils, sweat, and some wastes from the dermis to the skin's surface.
- Pigment in the dermis gives color to the skin.
- Nails and hair are part of the body covering system.
- The body covering system needs food, enough exercise, and rest to be kept healthy.

Science Words

body covering system	dermis	pores
skin	glands	pigment
epidermis		

Questions

1. How does your skin protect you?
2. From which layer of skin does bleeding occur when the skin is cut? Why?
3. Why is it important to clean your skin?
4. How does skin aid in cooling your body?
5. What causes color in your skin and hair?
6. Explain why the sun can be harmful to people with little pigment in their skin.
7. What would be a safe way to get a tan?
8. What causes skin to remain soft and smooth?
9. How do pores and glands help your skin?
10. Why are exercise, healthful food, and rest necessary for a healthy body covering system?

Chapter Two
Bones: Your Support System

What keeps this bridge from falling? In what way
is your body like this bridge? What supports your body?

All houses, buildings, and bridges need to be supported or held up so they do not fall. Your body also needs to be supported. What would happen if your body was not supported?

Skeleton

A skeleton is a hard structure that supports and protects an animal's body. Some invertebrates have skeletons on the outside of their bodies. The hard covering of insects and the shells of snails are types of skeletons. How does a skeleton help support and protect an insect?

Vertebrates have skeletons inside their bodies. Your skeleton is made mostly of bones which are inside your body. Your skeleton supports muscles and skin which cover it. What shape would you have without your skeleton?

Parts of the Skeleton

Bones are hard structures made of living cells and minerals. There are 206 bones in your skeleton. Your bones have different shapes and sizes. How are your leg bones and rib bones different? Bones are classified into four main groups: skull bones, backbones, trunk bones, and arm and leg bones.

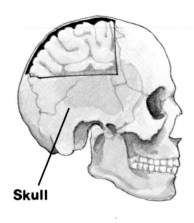

Skull

The skull is made of several bones. The **skull** surrounds the brain and gives shape to the head. How does the skull protect the brain? The cheek bones, part of the nose, and jaw bones are part of the skull, too.

The backbone, or spine, is made of 26 small, hollow bones. These bones are stacked on top of one another and form a tube that protects the nerves of the spinal cord. The spine helps support the body's weight and head.

The trunk or middle section of the skeleton is made of ribs and hipbones. Twelve pairs of ribs protect the heart and lungs like a cage. All the ribs

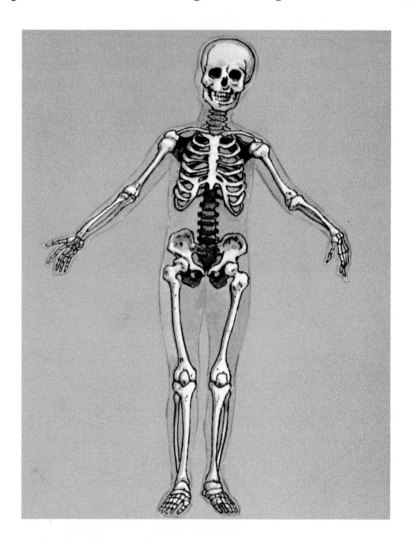

are connected to the upper spine. In the front, most of the ribs connect to the breastbone. Hipbones are connected to the lower spine. You can feel the top edge of the bowl-shaped hipbones. What body organs do the hipbones protect?

Arms and legs are made of long bones. Hands and feet are made of short bones. The large, thick leg bones provide support for the entire body. Many smaller bones form the wrists, ankles, fingers, and toes. The palm of each hand has five bones. Your fingers on one hand have 14 bones.

Feel the tip of your nose. Feel the outer parts of your ears. These parts of your skeleton are made of cartilage. It is also found where your bones join together. Cartilage has a smooth, spongelike property that cushions bones when you walk, run, or jump.

Healthy Bones

Your bones are alive! Blood vessels and nerves are in the center of some bones. The blood vessels allow blood to flow to the bone tissue. Blood contains the minerals and vitamins your bones need to grow and change. Your bones will grow larger until you are in your early twenties. A good diet will aid in keeping your bones healthy.

Activity

How Are Healthy and Unhealthy Bones Different?

What to use:

2 cleaned chicken bones   ½ liter of vinegar
2 jars with lids   pencil and paper
½ liter of water

What to do:

1. Observe both chicken bones. Try to bend and twist them but do not break them. Place a bone in each jar.

2. Fill one jar with enough vinegar to cover the one chicken bone. Fill the second jar with enough water to cover the second chicken bone.

3. Tightly cover both jars. Wait four or five days.

4. Remove both bones from the jars. Rinse them with water. Try to bend and twist each bone again.

What did you learn?

1. How did each chicken bone feel in step 1?
2. How did each chicken bone feel in step 4?

Using what you learned:

1. How are chicken bones like your bones?
2. How is the bone soaked in vinegar like an unhealthy bone?
3. How does the activity show what might happen if minerals were missing from your diet?
4. Why are minerals important for healthy bones?

Water

Vinegar

Your bones need minerals every day. Certain foods contain minerals and vitamins that make bones hard and strong. If you have a good diet, you will eat foods with enough minerals and vitamins.

Calcium (KAL see um) is one of the minerals that makes bones hard. A diet lacking in calcium will cause bones to become soft. Vitamin D is also necessary for hard bones. A good source of calcium and vitamin D is found in milk products. What milk products do you eat to keep your bones healthy?

Joints

Observe your arm, wrist, and hand while you move them. Each of these body parts has separate bones. Bones are joined together at places called **joints.** Each joint allows parts of the body to move in certain ways. Body joints include fixed joints, ball-and-socket joints, hinge joints, gliding joints, and pivot joints.

Feel your head. Your skull may feel and look like one big bone, but it is really several bones joined together. Look at the drawing. The skull bones join together at places called fixed joints. A fixed joint is a joint that moves very little. When you were a baby, the bones of your skull were not joined together. As you grew, the bones grew closer together. Now there are only small spaces called fixed joints between the bones. The small space is important to cushion any blows to the head.

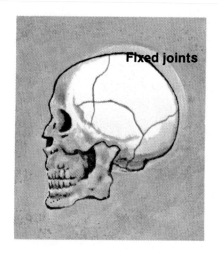
Fixed joints

Feel your shoulder as you move your whole arm around. Your shoulder is an example of a ball-and-socket joint. A ball-and-socket joint is a joint that allows the bones to move easily in a large circle. The joint is formed by the round end of a long bone fitting into a hole or socket of another bone.

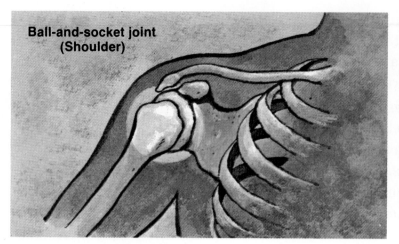

Ball-and-socket joint (Shoulder)

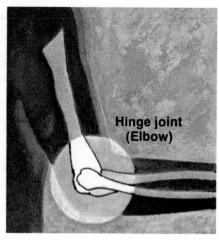

Hinge joint (Elbow)

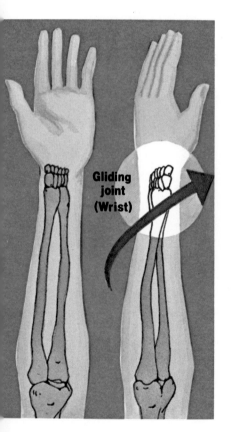

Gliding joint (Wrist)

The upper end of the arm bone has a round end. The shoulder bone has the socket in which the end of the arm bone fits. The other ball-and-socket joint in the body is the hip joint. What body parts does this ball-and-socket joint connect?

Now feel your knee. Watch how your knee moves when you bend it. How is this movement different from the movement of your entire leg? It is different because the joints are different. Remember, the kind of joint at the top of the leg is a ball-and-socket joint. The knee has a hinge joint. A hinge joint is a joint that allows movement back and forth. It is like a hinge on a door. How does a hinge on a door work? Look at the skeleton in the picture on page 128. What other body parts have hinge joints? When do you use your hinge joints?

The body has two other kinds of joints. Hold your arm out straight with your palm up. Move your lower arm and hand so that your palm is down. The wrist is a gliding joint that allows the bones to move in a twisting motion. Gliding joints are also found between the small bones in the spine. A pivot joint connects the head to the spine. It allows the head to move up and down as well as in a circle.

At each joint there are ligaments (LIHG uh munts). **Ligaments** are strong, tough fibers that hold bones together at the joints. A ligament looks like a cord and stretches easily to connect one bone to another bone across a joint. Ligaments also protect joints by keeping the bones from too much movement at the joints. If sudden movement occurs, ligaments can become stretched or torn causing a sprain. A **sprain** is a condition that occurs when ligaments tear or stretch away from the bones.

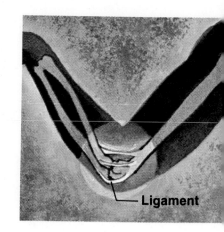
Ligament

Making Sure

1. What do bone tissues need to stay healthy?
2. How is the ball-and-socket joint like a pivot joint?
3. How do ligaments protect joints?

Broken Bones

What should you do if you break a bone? A crack or break in a bone is called a **fracture** (FRAK chur). How do you think a fracture feels? How would you know if your bone were broken?

It is important to see a doctor right away if you think you have a broken bone. The doctor checks to see where and how the bone is broken. The doctor might find out whether the bone is broken by feeling the body part that covers the bone. An X ray of the bone might be taken. If the bone is broken, the doctor can see the fracture in an X ray. The doctor will set or move the broken pieces of the bone back into the right position. If the fracture is not set correctly, the bone may not heal well or grow straight.

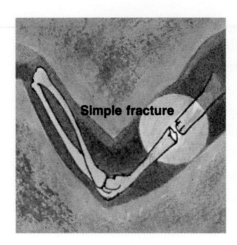

Simple fracture

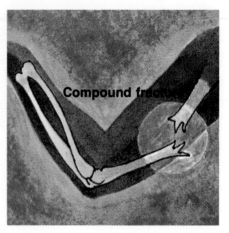

Compound fracture

A hard, stiff covering called a cast may be placed around the fracture after the bone is set. A cast is almost like an outside skeleton. The cast keeps the broken pieces of bone from moving so the fracture can heal. The fracture heals by forming new cartilage which later changes to bone. It may take from four weeks to a year for a bone to heal. The healing time depends on the size of the broken bone, the age of the person, and the type of fracture.

There are two types of fractures, simple and compound. A simple fracture is a break in the bone. A compound fracture is a break in both the bone and skin. The skin break is caused by the broken end of the bone coming through the skin. How would you know whether someone has a compound fracture?

Chapter Review

Summary

- The skeleton is the support system of the body.
- The skeleton supports, protects, and helps move the body.
- Bones join together at places called joints.
- The joints of the body affect bone movement.
- Ligaments stretch to allow bones to move at the joints but keep bones from moving too much.
- A sprain occurs if ligaments are stretched or torn from the bones.
- A fracture is a broken bone.
- There are simple and compound fractures.

Science Words

bones	**joints**	**sprain**
skull	**ligaments**	**fracture**
calcium		

Questions

1. Why is our skeleton necessary?
2. What does the skull protect?
3. What might happen to your bones if enough minerals were left out of your diet?
4. What foods supply your bones with calcium?
5. Name the kinds of joints in the body.
6. Give an example of each of the kinds of joints.
7. What kind of joint allows you to turn your head?
8. What kind of joint allows you to chew your food?
9. How is your knee joint like the hinge on a door?
10. How are ligaments important to joints?

Chapter Three

Muscles: The Body Movers

What moves your skeleton? How are you able to move the parts of your body? How do you walk, run, and move like the young people in the picture? How do parts inside your body move?

You have more than 400 different special tissues to move your bones! These special tissues also make parts of your body work. These special tissues are called muscles.

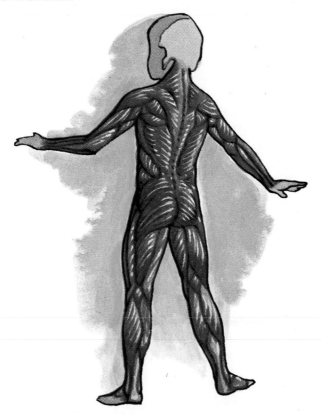

What Are Muscles?

Muscles are special tissues that move body parts and form and shape your body. What part of your body has a large amount of muscle? Muscles protect your body. They can cushion a bump and allow you to move away from danger.

Muscles that surround your bones are the workers of the body. Move your head from side to side. Muscles like those in your neck are voluntary (VAHL un ter ee) muscles. **Voluntary muscles** move when you think about moving them. You had to think to move your head. Most of the muscles surrounding your bones are voluntary muscles. How do you know the muscles in your arm are voluntary?

Many body organs have muscles, too. These organ muscles are called involuntary (ihn VAHL un ter ee) muscles. **Involuntary muscles** work or move on their own. You do not have to think about moving them to make them move. Involuntary muscles make many of the movements necessary to keep you alive. They control your breathing and your heartbeat. They also move food through your body during digestion.

At times, voluntary muscles can act like involuntary muscles. When you are cold, some of your voluntary muscles cause you to shiver. You have no control over them until you become warm. Why do you think the voluntary muscles act on their own when you are cold?

Cardiac Muscle

Try to feel a movement in the left side of your chest. What organ do you think is causing the movement? Your heart is a special kind of involuntary muscle called **cardiac** (KARD ee ak) **muscle.** Your cardiac muscle has been working on its own since before your birth. It has always been pumping blood through your body. Your cardiac muscle beats more than 100,000 times each day. Each contracting, or squeezing, and relaxing of the cardiac muscle is one heartbeat. It can rest briefly only between heartbeats. What might happen if this involuntary muscle stopped working?

Smooth Muscles

The involuntary muscles of your other body organs are called **smooth muscles.** Smooth muscles are part of your organs. For example, smooth muscles in the walls of your stomach move food as you digest it. Then the stomach's smooth muscles push the food into the small intestine.

Cardiac muscle

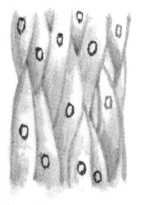

Smooth muscle

Like the cardiac muscle, you do not have to think about making your smooth muscles work. Why is it good that you do not have to think about moving them? What might happen if the smooth muscles in your stomach did not work after you ate?

Skeletal Muscles

Skeletal muscle

Feel your arm. You can feel skin and the hardness of your bone. The tissue between your skin and bone is skeletal (SKEL ut ul) muscle. **Skeletal muscles** surround the bones, allowing you to move your bones. You use skeletal muscles to run and jump.

You can control your skeletal muscles. They are voluntary muscles. An ice skater moves over the ice by controlling the skeletal muscles. The skater must think about moving arm, leg, and head muscles. These muscles move when the skater wants them to move.

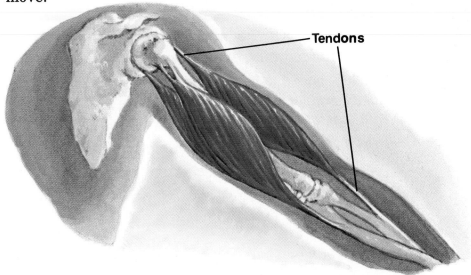

Tendons

Skeletal muscles are attached to your bones by tendons (TEN dunz). **Tendons** are tough, white tissues that attach muscles to bones. Tendons are usually short and do not stretch. You can see tendons near your knuckles when you make a fist. How many do you see when you make a fist?

Activity

How Do Skeletal Muscles Move?

What to use:

your muscles

pencil and paper

What to do:

1. Place your right hand on the front of your left upper arm.

2. Raise your left lower arm slowly. Your left arm should bend at the elbow. Do this several times and observe what happens.

3. Now place your right hand on the back of your left upper arm. Repeat step 2.

What did you learn?

1. What happens to the muscles on the front of your upper arm as you raise the lower arm?

2. What happens to the muscles on the front of your upper arm as you lower the lower arm?

3. What happens to the muscles on the back of your upper arm as you raise the lower arm?

4. What happens to the muscles on the back of your upper arm as you lower the lower arm?

Using what you learned:

1. Which arm muscles cause the arm to straighten?

2. What kinds of exercise would help you strengthen your upper arm muscles?

3. What kinds of exercise would you do to strengthen your upper leg muscles? Which body parts would be moving the most in these exercises?

4. Which leg muscles cause the leg to straighten?

How Muscles Work

Muscles work by being contracted (kun TRAKT ud). A **contracted muscle** is a muscle that becomes tighter and shorter. To make your lower arm move up, the front upper arm muscle contracts. The contracted muscle pulls on the lower arm bone to make the arm move up. What happens to the thickness of your upper arm muscle as it contracts?

When you straighten your arm, the muscle relaxes. A **relaxed muscle** is one that is looser and longer than a contracted muscle. What happens to the thickness of your upper arm muscle as it relaxes?

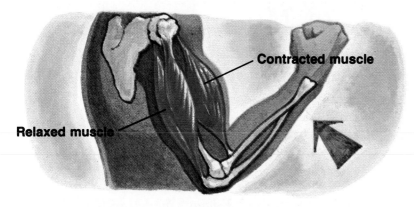

Skeletal muscles work in pairs to move a bone. As one muscle of the pair contracts, the other muscle relaxes. When you bend your arm at the elbow, the top muscle of your upper arm contracts. You can feel it shorten and tighten as it is pulling on the lower arm. The muscle under your upper arm becomes relaxed. It is looser and longer.

When you straighten your arm, the top muscle of your upper arm lengthens. It is relaxed and is not pulling. The muscle under your upper arm contracts. It becomes shorter and pulls on your lower arm to straighten the arm. These two muscles work together to move your lower arm. Pairs of skeletal muscles all over your body contract and relax to move your body. When one muscle on a bone contracts, the other relaxes.

If muscles are overused, they may cramp. When muscles cramp, they contract without your control. A cramp is painful. When you get a cramp, rub the muscle. Rubbing will help relax the muscle and ease the pain.

Making Sure

1. What is the difference between contracted and relaxed muscles?
2. What voluntary muscles does a weight lifter use?

Care of Muscles

Study the pictures carefully. How are muscles being used here? How are cardiac and skeletal muscles being used? Exercise strengthens the muscles and keeps them in good health. Without enough exercise, muscles become weak. Daily exercise makes the muscles strong and the body healthy. Exercise is important for the health of the whole body. Swimming, skating, bicycling, skiing, walking, and running are some ways to exercise. Exercise helps muscles grow and work properly.

Perhaps you have seen someone who wore a cast for a long time. He or she was not able to exercise the muscles under the cast. Those muscles became

weak and smaller. Soon after the muscles were exercised, they became strong and healthy again. What are your favorite forms of exercise? Why is it important for people of all ages to exercise?

Rest and sleep are important for healthy muscles, too. Suppose you did not rest your muscles before using them. If your muscles hurt, what do you think caused them to hurt? Muscles used for a long time, without rest, become very tired and sore.

Good eating habits make muscles strong. Muscles are living tissues and require a healthful diet to grow and work well. Find out how important diet is to athletes. How important is diet to you?

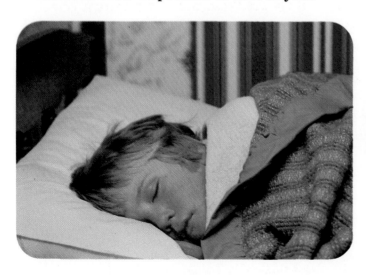

Everyone Is a Winner!

Exercise is important for good health. Taking part in your favorite sport is a fun way to exercise. You may wonder how children with a handicap exercise. They enjoy many of the same sports you do!

Swimming, bowling, and ice skating are popular. Children with a handicap enjoy some special sports, too. They compete in wheelchair races and frisbee contests!

The Special Olympics are major sports events just for people with handicaps. Many people compete in Special Olympic contests around the world. These people exercise and practice each day. Some practice as a team. Others practice to compete alone. Preparing for the contests is hard work, but it is lots of fun, too.

Everyone likes to win a contest. It's great to win after working hard and long. At the Special Olympics, everyone is a winner. Even without winning first place, everyone wins better health through daily exercise.

Chapter Review

Summary

- Muscles move parts of the body.
- Voluntary muscles are muscles you control.
- Involuntary muscles are muscles that work on their own.
- Cardiac muscle is the heart muscle.
- Smooth muscles make up the organs of the body.
- Skeletal muscles are voluntary muscles that move bones.
- Tendons attach skeletal muscles to bones.
- Exercise, rest, and a healthful diet are important in keeping muscles firm and strong.

Science Words

muscles	skeletal muscles
voluntary muscles	tendons
involuntary muscles	contracted muscle
cardiac muscle	relaxed muscle
smooth muscles	

Questions

1. Describe what each type of muscle does.
2. Tell which muscle types are voluntary.
3. How are tendons important for bone movement?
4. Name a way to speed up the cardiac muscle.
5. Explain how a pair of skeletal muscles works.
6. What type of muscles do you use to pedal your bike, voluntary or involuntary?
7. How do you take good care of your muscles?
8. Where are smooth muscles found?
9. Where are skeletal muscles found?
10. What muscles do you use to throw a softball, voluntary or involuntary?

Chapter Four

Nerves: The Message System

How do you send messages to a friend? Why does your body send messages? What communication system is in your body?

Like the telephone company and the post office, you have a communication system. It is inside your body. This system carries messages to and from all parts of your body. With these messages, you sense and respond to your environment. This system controls how your body parts work.

Brain

The communication system of the body is called the **nervous** (NUR vus) **system.** The nervous system is made of the brain, spinal (SPINE ul) cord, and nerves. These parts work together to carry messages throughout your body.

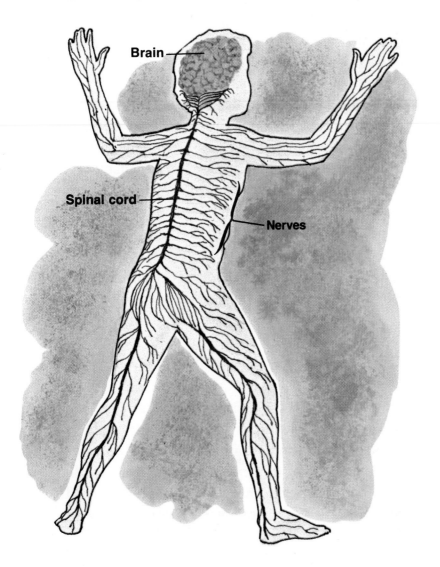

Brain

Spinal cord

Nerves

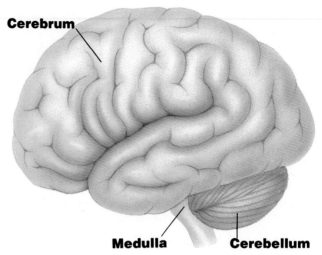

Cerebrum

Medulla   Cerebellum

The **brain** is the main control center of the body and the nervous system. The brain controls the body by receiving and sending messages. Messages coming to the brain report what is needed by the body. Messages sent by the brain take care of body needs. In addition to thinking, reasoning, and remembering, the brain can also control body movement.

Your brain has three main areas. The top part of the brain is called the cerebrum (suh REE brum). The **cerebrum** is the part of the brain that controls your thinking, learning, and talking. The cerebrum controls your five senses and your memory. It is the part of the brain that helps you remember what you learned so you can do well on a test.

Just below the back part of the cerebrum is the cerebellum (ser uh BEL um). The **cerebellum** is the part of the brain that controls the voluntary muscles of the body. Throwing a ball, petting your dog, or riding a bike are controlled by the cerebellum.

There is a third part of the brain that controls involuntary muscles. It is the medulla (muh DUL uh). The **medulla** is the bottom part of the brain that controls some involuntary muscles. It controls the muscles for breathing, heartbeat, and digestion. If the medulla is damaged, a person will usually die.

Death occurs because the involuntary muscles do not receive the message to work. Suppose someone were choking. Which part of the brain would control the coughing?

Making Sure

1. How is your nervous system like a telephone system?
2. What are the three main parts of the brain?

Spinal Cord and Nerves

Connected to the medulla is a large group of nerves forming the spinal cord. The **spinal cord** is a thick, cordlike bundle of nerve cells. Messages travel along the spinal cord to and from the brain. The spinal cord is part of a communication system within the body.

Look at the drawing of the human nervous system on page 147. Notice where the spinal cord is located. Trace how a message travels from the finger to the brain. What would happen to the body's communication system if the spinal cord were injured?

Nerves are threadlike cells throughout the body that carry messages to and from the brain. Nerves carry messages from the body parts through the spinal cord and into the brain. They also carry messages from the brain through the spinal cord to the body parts. Nerves in the body are like telephone wires that go from the main office to each house. They also go from each house to the main office. Like telephone calls, you can send or receive messages to and from all parts of your body.

You may sense a soft kitten by touching it with your hand. The brain understands the message as soft.

You will not know the kitten is soft until nerves carry the message to the brain. When messages are sent from any body part to your brain, you are sensing. Nerves that carry a message from a body part to the brain are called **sensory** (SENS uh ree) **nerves.** Sensory nerves receive messages from both outside and inside the body. These nerves allow you to sense the environment and your body. What messages did your sensory nerves send about today's weather?

Often sensory nerves cause the action of your motor nerves. **Motor nerves** are nerves that carry messages from the brain to the muscles. Motor nerves cause the muscles to contract. When the muscles contract, action takes place. Your voluntary muscles work when you think about doing a task. If you want to raise your hand, a message is sent from the brain through the motor nerves. The motor nerves in your shoulder and arm carry the message to the muscles. Your muscles receive the message and you lift your arm. All this happens in less than one second.

Some of the body movements you make are done without your thinking about them. A **reflex** (REE fleks) is a special action that involves only the nerves and the spinal cord. A reflex happens without thinking about it. A reflex may help protect you from injury.

Activity

What Is a Reflex?

What to use:

your hand

a partner

pencil and paper

What to do:

1. Have your partner look straight ahead.

2. Quickly wave your hand 10 cm in front of your partner's eyes. Observe your partner's eyes.

What did you learn?

1. What did you observe when you waved your hand?

2. Ask your partner whether or not he or she thought about blinking.

Using what you learned:

1. How does a reflex act protect you?

2. What other reflex acts do you have?

Reflexes Protect People

Some messages take a shortcut. Certain reflexes travel only to the spinal cord. In the spinal cord, a message is crossed over from a sensory nerve to a motor nerve. The action, such as moving your hand away from a needle, takes place without the message going to the brain. In what way does a reflex act help your body?

One day Mike was frying an egg. The pan became hot and the egg started to burn. Mike grabbed the pan with his bare hand. What did Mike feel? What type of nerve messages occurred?

Mike let go of the pan as soon as he touched it. A sensory message went from Mike's fingers to his spinal cord. In the spinal cord, the message was passed from the sensory nerves to the motor nerves. The motor nerves made Mike's arm and hand muscles contract. These muscles caused the fingers to open and made Mike let go of the pan. How did letting go of the pan protect Mike?

Mike let go of the pan before he realized what was happening. Nerve messages were also sent up the spinal cord into the cerebrum. Mike felt the pain when

the message reached his brain. What other sense allowed Mike to realize something was happening?

Mike's action was a reflex. A reflex allowed him to react fast. The nerve message went to the spinal cord and back to the muscles. If the message had to go to the brain first, it would have taken a longer time. What would happen to Mike's hand if the message took a longer time?

Drugs and the Nervous System

Some substances change the way the nervous system works. These substances are called drugs. **Drugs** are chemicals that cause a change in the body. Drugs may speed up or slow down the messages passing through the nervous system. Certain chemicals in cocoa, coffee, tea, and some soft drinks are drugs. Aspirin and toothpaste have drugs in them. Medicines doctors prescribe contain drugs.

Whether drugs are helpful or harmful depends on how they are used. A doctor can prescribe a certain amount of drug to deaden pain or cure an infection. What experience have you had with a pain-killing drug at the dentist? Used in a controlled way, the right amount of a drug can be helpful to you.

Using too much of a drug, or using the drug too often, may be dangerous. For example, some people use drugs to go to sleep when they cannot fall asleep on their own. Use of sleeping pills, or any drug taken too often, can cause the body to depend on the drug. It is healthier for your body to relax in a natural way. What can you do when you want to relax or go to sleep?

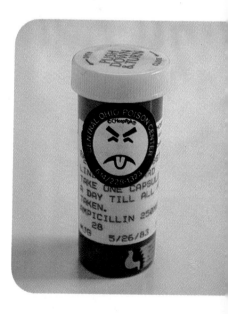

Whenever you use a drug, you should follow the directions on the label completely. Labels on medicines always explain how to use the drugs.

You can help with drug safety by keeping drugs and medicines away from young children. Safety labels can be placed on drugs and medicines to warn young children. Have an adult help read the label before taking any medicine. What else can you do to prevent young children from taking these drugs accidentally?

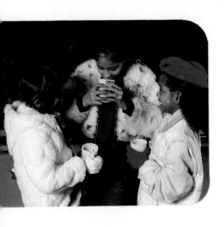

Not all drugs are medicines. Some soft drinks, coffee, tea, and cocoa contain the drug caffeine (ka FEEN). **Caffeine** is a drug that speeds up the nervous system. It increases the heartbeat and the pressure of the blood against the walls of the blood vessels. The nervous system is changed for a time. People may become nervous from too much caffeine.

Another common drug is nicotine (NIHK uh teen). **Nicotine** is a drug found in tobacco. Like caffeine, nicotine speeds up the nervous system.

Alcohol (AL kuh hawl) is a drug that slows down the nervous system. Some people drink beverages with alcohol in them. Too much alcohol will slow down reflexes. Sometimes slow reflexes may cause harm. Why is it important for people not to drive after drinking alcohol?

Over the years, scientists have learned more about using drugs to treat illnesses. Drugs can be helpful if taken with care. To get the most help from drugs, it is important to know how drugs can affect your body.

Chapter Review

Summary

- The nervous system is the communication system of the body.
- The brain, spinal cord, and nerves make up the nervous system.
- The cerebrum, cerebellum, and medulla are parts of the brain working together to perform different tasks.
- The spinal cord carries messages to and from the brain.
- Nerves carry messages from body parts through the spinal cord to the brain.
- The motor and sensory nerves work to relay messages.
- Reflexes are one way the body protects itself.
- Drugs can affect the nervous system.

Science Words

nervous system	spinal cord	drugs
brain	nerves	caffeine
cerebrum	sensory nerves	nicotine
cerebellum	motor nerves	alcohol
medulla	reflex	

Questions

1. Name the three parts of the nervous system.
2. Why is a reflex important?
3. Which parts of the brain work to help you write?
4. What are the "main wires" of the nervous system?
5. What are the "smaller wires" of the nervous system?
6. Why is your spinal cord important?
7. What happens when a spinal cord is damaged?
8. How are sensory nerves different from motor nerves?
9. Name two drugs which speed up the nervous system.
10. What are the dangers of using drugs?

Self Checks

Answer these Self Checks on a sheet of paper.

1. What should you do so all of your body systems work well and stay healthy?

2. How do voluntary muscles work in pairs?

3. What is the communication system of the body?

4. Name these joints. Which one allows the most movement? Which allows the least movement?

a

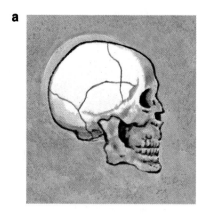

b

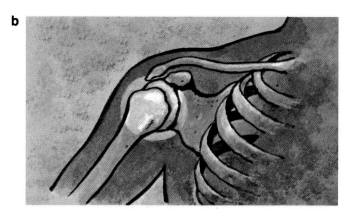

c

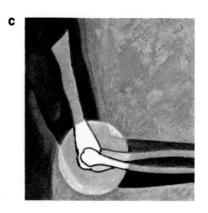

d

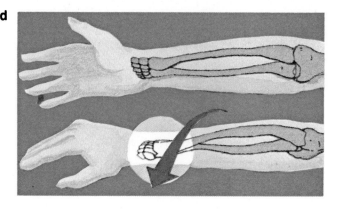

Idea Corner

More Fun with Science

1. Have a friend draw the outline of your body on a large sheet of paper. Obtain pictures of the human bone and muscle systems. Draw and label some of the bones and muscles.

2. Make a chart that has a list of exercises on it. Test and record the physical fitness of each class member as each exercise is done.

3. Obtain a cooked chicken leg. Carefully cut away part of the skin and meat. Determine which are the muscles, ligaments, and tendons. Identify the joints you see.

4. Visit a person who takes X-ray pictures. Have them explain the body parts you can see in the X-ray pictures.

5. Make a hinge joint model. Use a metal hinge, two large rubber bands, and two boards (for bones) to demonstrate how the lower arm is raised.

Reading for Fun

Facts About the Human Body by Marianne Tully and Mary-Alice Tully, Franklin Watts, Inc.: New York, © 1977.
   What causes hiccups? Learn the answer to this and many more questions.

The Kids' Diet Cookbook by Aileen Paul, Doubleday & Company, Inc.: Garden City, NY, © 1980.
   Are you interested in eating well and feeling great? Read this book to learn how to plan and prepare healthful and delicious meals.

The Natural Snack Cookbook by Jill Pinkwater, Four Winds Press: New York, © 1975.

Unit 5

Motion, Force, and Work

Chapter One
From Here to There

How do you know this person is moving? What causes objects to move? How fast do they move?

People and objects are moving all the time. They move from place to place. They speed up, slow down, and change directions. How have you moved today? What objects are moving in your classroom now?

Where Are You?

To find people and objects, we need to know their positions. **Position** is the place where you are or where an object is. What is your position right now? To describe your position, you must give enough information so someone else could find you.

Suppose you are riding in a car with your father when he gets lost. He looks at a map to find which way to go. Why is it important for your father to know his position on the map? Why is it important for your father to know the position of where he wants to go?

If you are on a softball team, why is it important for you to know the position of first base? What other positions in softball are important to know?

Changing Position

When you move from one position to another, you are in motion. **Motion** is changing position.

Motion cannot occur without a force. **Force** is a push or pull. What force did you use to get to school?

Sir Isaac Newton (1642–1727) studied position, motion, and force. He observed that a force is needed to change the motion of all objects. Newton also learned that once an object is in motion, it continues in motion until another force acts on it. Your bicycle does not move until you apply a force to the pedals. Once in motion, the bicycle continues in motion until you put on the brakes. How does applying the brakes on the bicycle change its motion?

Often gravity causes an object to change direction. When you bat a ball, the force of your muscles puts the ball in motion and changes the ball's direction. The ball falls to the ground if no one catches it. What force causes the ball to fall to the ground? In the picture below, what force will act on the ball? How will the force change the position and motion of the ball?

Newton called the force and change of motion the first law of motion. The **first law of motion** states that objects at rest stay at rest and objects in motion stay in motion unless acted on by a force. You can see the effects of the first law of motion every day. Look around your classroom. Notice the books and papers lying there. When will they move? What forces can make them move?

A force is used any time an object begins moving, stops moving, or changes direction. Forces can start an object moving or speed up an object that is already moving. Forces can slow down, stop, or change the direction of a moving object.

How Fast Are Motions?

Speed is a measure of how fast an object moves. Speeds may be very fast, very slow, or medium. A jet plane flying at 1000 kilometers per hour is moving at a very fast speed. A snail moving at 5 meters per hour is moving at a very slow speed. What are some medium speeds?

You can find the speed of an object. Divide the distance the object moves by the amount of time it takes the object to move that distance.

$$\text{Speed} = \text{Distance} \div \text{Time}$$

Speed can be measured in centimeters per second, meters per year, or any units of distance and time.

Suppose you are going by car to see a friend who lives far away. You know that the distance from your home to your friend's home is 150 km. It takes two hours in a car for you to get to your friend's home. You can find the speed of the car.

$$\text{Speed} = \text{Distance} \div \text{Time}$$
$$\text{Speed} = 150 \text{ kilometers} \div 2 \text{ hours}$$
$$\text{Speed} = 75 \text{ kilometers per hour}$$

Imagine that you go for a bicycle ride with your friends. You ride for three hours. If you ride 48 km, what is your riding speed?

Activity

What Is Your Walking Speed?

What to use:

watch or clock   large area for walking
meter stick   pencil and paper
masking tape

What to do:

1. With the meter stick, measure 10 meters on the floor. Mark the distance with masking tape.

2. Have one person walk the 10-meter distance five times. Use the clock to find out how long this takes. Time yourself and several other people walking the same distance.

3. Use pencil and paper to record the total time for each person.

4. Divide the total distance by each person's total time to find the walking speed of each person.

What did you learn?

1. What is your walking speed?
2. How is your walking speed different from the walking speeds of your friends?
3. Why did you have each person walk 5 times?

Using what you learned:

1. At your walking speed, how long would it take you to walk 500 meters?
2. How could you find your running speed?

Changing Speed

Speed changes when the motion of the object changes. **Acceleration** (ak sel uh RAY shun) is an increase in the speed of an object. A race car can accelerate fast. It accelerates faster than most family cars because it has a greater force.

Suppose you are pulling a wagon full of newspapers. What happens to the acceleration of the wagon if a friend helps? Why is the direction of the force on the wagon important? What happens to the wagon's acceleration if your friend pulls in a different direction?

Isaac Newton studied the acceleration of objects and wrote the second law of motion. The **second law of motion** states that an object's acceleration depends on the mass of the object and the size and direction of the force acting on it.

Activity

How Does Mass Affect Acceleration?

What to use:

string	"Puller Pal"
paper clip	3 chalkboard erasers

What to do:

1. Using the "Puller Pal," slowly pull three erasers across a table as shown in the picture.

2. Record the amount of force needed to accelerate the three erasers by placing a mark on the "Puller Pal."

3. Remove one of the erasers. Pull the remaining two erasers across the table using the *same amount* of force as you used in step 1.

4. Repeat step 1 again using only one eraser. Try to use the *same amount* of force.

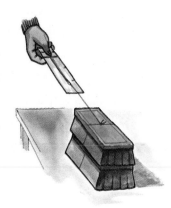

What did you learn?

1. What happened to the acceleration as you used fewer erasers?
2. What was being decreased as you used fewer erasers?
3. How does mass affect acceleration?

Using what you learned:

1. Why are bicycle racers concerned about how lightweight their bikes are?
2. Why do some very long freight trains have more than one engine?
3. Why do race cars have more powerful engines than family cars?

The acceleration of the object also depends on the mass of the object. It would be difficult for you to push a wagon with a lot of mass. The wagon would not be able to accelerate fast. More force is needed to accelerate an object with more mass.

Why is a roller coaster ride exciting? A roller coaster is a good example of acceleration and deceleration (dee sel uh RAY shun). **Deceleration** is a decrease in the speed of an object. You may have felt the pushes and pulls of acceleration and deceleration as the roller coaster went up, down, and around. What other examples of acceleration and deceleration might you find at an amusement park? What examples might you find on a playground?

People and objects are moved from location to location by forces. Forces start or stop an object. They can speed up an object or change the direction of an object already in motion.

Making Sure

1. How are motion and speed different?
2. If you throw a ball as hard as you can, what forces act on the ball?

Opposite Forces

Two teams in a tug-of-war contest pull on a rope in opposite directions. Each team uses force. The forces of the teams are in opposite directions.

Some forces are strong. Other forces are weak. In a tug-of-war, there will be no change of motion as long as the two teams pull with the same strength or force. Neither team will win. What if one team is stronger? Which team was stronger in the picture? Changes of motion only happen when one force is stronger than the opposite force.

Newton's Third Law of Motion

Jessica was roller skating one day. She stopped when she came to a brick wall. Jessica faced the wall and pushed on it with her hands. She rolled backwards on her skates away from the wall. Newton's third law of motion describes Jessica's motion after pushing on the wall. The **third law of motion** states that for every action force there is an equal and opposite reaction force. The action force was Jessica's push on the wall. The reaction force was the wall's push on Jessica.

People and Science

Who Cares?

Who cares about motion and force? Police officers do! Police officers learn about motion and force in police training school. They learn how to collect useful evidence. Knowing about motion and force helps.

When traffic accidents occur, police officers work quickly to collect useful information. They may photograph or map the accident scene. This records the exact locations of the autos. The officers measure skid marks caused by friction between tires and the road. Police officers know that this information can be used to find the deceleration of the autos. The force of the crash may tell the speed or acceleration of the autos.

Police scientists study the information that police officers collect. With the right information, police scientists can find out how and why accidents happen. Perhaps other accidents can be prevented.

Chapter Review

Summary

- You are in motion when you move from one position to another.
- Speed is a measure of how fast an object moves.
- A force is a push or a pull.
- Acceleration is an increase in speed.
- Deceleration is a decrease in speed.
- An object stays at rest unless some force puts it in motion.
- The acceleration of an object depends on its mass and the size and direction of the force acting on it.
- For every action force there is an equal and opposite reaction force.

Science Words

position	first law of motion	second law of motion
motion	speed	deceleration
force	acceleration	third law of motion

Questions

1. Why are position and motion important to people?
2. What is the speed of a runner who runs a 100-meter race in 20 seconds?
3. A car approaches a stop sign and stops. It then moves on. Describe this in terms of deceleration and acceleration.
4. What causes motion to change?
5. Why will a certain force cause some objects to move but not others?
6. In your own words, explain Newton's three laws of motion.
7. A person standing in a wagon jumps out the back. The wagon and person move in opposite directions. Two laws of motion are at work. What are they? Explain.
8. Why do smaller, lighter cars use less fuel? How is this an example of one of the laws of motion?

Chapter Two

Forces and Your World

What are the forces in this picture? Where are they found? Why are forces important to you?

Forces are a very important part of your world. You use forces when you work and play. What could you do if there were no forces? You could not play ball. You could not ride a bicycle. You could not talk on the telephone with a friend. You could not watch television. There would be no electric lights for reading at night. You could not pour a glass of milk for a bedtime snack. Without forces, your world would be very different.

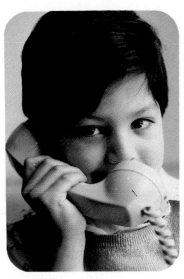
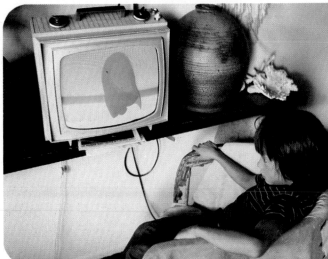

Forces are all around you. Sometimes forces act together. Sometimes they act against each other. Some forces hold objects together. Other forces keep objects apart. Why do you think it is important to learn about the forces in your world? What forces can you identify in the pictures on this page?

Friction

Imagine you are riding a bike on a flat surface. You pedal very hard and very fast. Then you stop pedaling. You are coasting. What happens? You keep coasting as long as you can. Finally your bicycle comes to a stop. Why did your bike stop?

The first law of motion states that a moving object keeps moving until it is acted on by some force. Your coasting on a bicycle was stopped by a force. This force is known as friction (FRIHK shun). **Friction** is a force that slows down and stops moving objects. Friction occurs when two objects slide or roll across each other.

If you roll a ball and let it go, the ball will slow down and stop. Why does the ball slow down and stop? A force must have stopped the ball, but what force? The ball stopped rolling because of friction. There was friction between the ball and the ground and between the ball and the air. Where is friction acting when you are coasting on a bicycle?

The surface of any object has tiny bumps and holes in it. If you could look at the surface of an object through a microscope, you could see bumps. Look at the picture here. It shows the surface of an egg with a tiny crack. You can see the surface does not look smooth. Friction occurs as the bumps and holes of two surfaces catch and rub together.

When the surfaces are rubbed together, heat is produced. Friction causes heat. Rub your hands together. What is causing the heat? The action of friction also wears away the surfaces of objects.

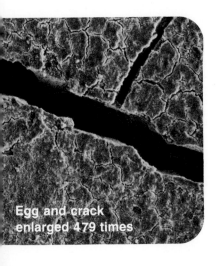

Egg and crack enlarged 479 times

Think about the stones found near a beach. Why are they smooth? What do you think wore away their surfaces? Look at the bottoms of your shoes. What area has been worn away? Look around your classroom. What other examples of friction wearing away surfaces are there?

Friction can be useful. You use friction every day. You could not walk without friction. Friction between your shoes and the floor allows you to move. There is very little friction between your shoes and a smooth floor. That is why you tend to slip. If there were no friction, you would not be able to walk!

Without friction, many everyday activities would not be possible. Without friction, you would not be able to write your name or draw a picture. Why would it be impossible to do these activities without friction? What else would be impossible without friction?

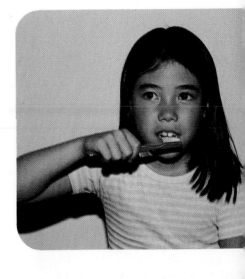

Friction can be a problem, too. Moving parts of machines are worn away by friction. The worn machine parts must be replaced. In machines, such as car engines, oil is used to reduce the amount of friction. Oil helps to reduce the wearing of the moving machine parts. What other ways can you think of that people use to reduce friction? How else can friction be a problem?

1. What causes friction?
2. Why do people rub the runners of their snow sleds with steel wool or wax their snow skis?

Magnetic and Electric Forces

Magnets cause a force in the area around them. The area of force around magnets is called a **magnetic field.** You cannot see a magnetic field but you can see what it does. What happens if you place an iron nail near a magnet?

The Earth also has a magnetic field. The Earth is surrounded by magnetic lines of force. The girls here are making use of these magnetic lines of force in order to check their position. What instrument are they using?

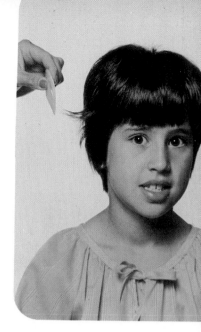

Another force you cannot see is electric force. When objects with electric charges are near each other, they attract or repel. The pull or push of electric charges is an **electric force.** You may have seen what an electric force can do. Sometimes when you comb your hair, a few hairs are pulled toward the comb. Your hair and the comb have electric charges. The electric force forms a field like the field around magnets.

People have learned to use electric and magnetic forces. Electric lights, television, and telephones use magnetic and electric forces. How are magnetic and electric forces important to you?

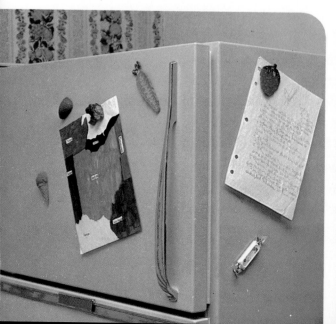

Gravity

Another important force in our world is gravity (GRAV ut ee). **Gravity** is the pulling force of every object on all other objects. You cannot see gravity, but you can see what it does. If you throw an object into the air, it will fall to the ground. The Earth's gravity causes the object to change direction and fall down. The Earth's gravity keeps objects from going up forever.

Every object has gravity forces. The amount of pulling force depends on the mass of the objects and their distance from each other. Objects with a larger mass have a larger force. Objects with a smaller mass have a smaller force. The force of an object with a small mass is so slight that we do not notice its effects. Why is the Earth's gravity so great?

Distance between objects also affects the pulling force of gravity. In this way, gravity is similar to the force of a magnet. The farther away objects are from

a magnet, the weaker the force. The force of gravity between two objects also becomes less as the two objects are moved away from each other. How can spacecraft get beyond the Earth's gravity? Why does a ball thrown high into the air not escape the pulling force of the Earth?

Gravity is very important to the way we live. What would have to be different in your classroom if there were no gravity? Sometimes gravity can be a problem. People fall down because of gravity. Objects with a lot of mass are hard to move because of gravity. We still need gravity! Look at the pictures on this page. What benefits are people getting from gravity?

Forces and Pressure

Objects can apply a force against other objects. The objects can be either solids, liquids, or gases. Pressure is related to the pushing force of objects. Pressure is also related to the area on which the object is pushing.

Pressure is a measure of the amount of force applied to a certain area. While standing on the floor with both feet, the weight of your body applies force to a certain area on the floor. This causes pressure on the floor. What happens to the pressure on the floor if you stand on one foot? Why? What happens to the pressure on the floor if you lie down?

Liquids push against objects, also. You can feel the pressure of water in a garden hose. Imagine you are holding a garden hose. What do you feel when the water is turned off? What do you feel when the water is turned on? If the water is turned on fully, how can you increase the water pressure to make the water squirt out farther?

Gases also push against objects. We use air to fill tires. The air pushes outward in all directions against the inside of the tire. The pressure of the air on the inside of the tire provides enough force to support the weight of a car or truck. What happens when a tire goes flat?

Gas pressure is very useful. Some products are packaged in pressurized spray cans. The gas pressure inside a spray can is greater than the air pressure outside the can. Therefore, the liquid inside the can is pushed out when you press down on the nozzle. How have you used gas pressure?

Activity

How Can You See Air Pressure Clues?

What to use:
large, widemouth jar
plastic bag
rubber band
pencil and paper

What to do:
1. Place the plastic bag inside the jar.

2. Bring the edges out over the top of the jar and seal tightly with rubber bands.

3. Reach inside and try to pull the bottom part of the plastic bag to the outside of the jar. Observe and record what happens.

What did you learn?
1. What happened when you tried to pull the bag out of the jar?
2. What force was acting on the bag?

Using what you learned:
1. What would happen if you poked a hole in the plastic bag?
2. Would it be easier or harder to pull the bag out of a larger jar? Why?

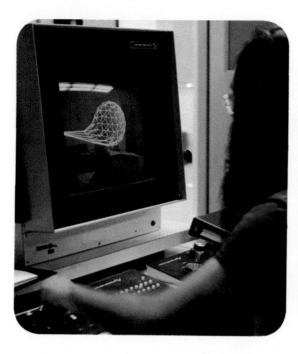

Your world has forces that allow you to perform actions. The same forces prevent you from performing other actions. Friction, magnetic and electric forces, and gravity are forces you can sense. Some of these forces you can measure. The photographs illustrate electric and magnetic forces, gravity, and friction. How can you use these forces?

Sidewalk Surfing

Perhaps you have been sidewalk surfing without knowing it. Sidewalk surfing is also known as skateboarding. You may think skateboarding is a new sport, but it began in the 1950s. Some surfers in California wanted to try a new sport. They nailed roller skate wheels to pieces of wood and began "sidewalk surfing." Skateboards have been improved since the 1950s. The improvements helped skateboarding become a popular sport.

Gravity and friction are important forces for skateboard riders. The pull of the Earth's gravity helps skateboard riders gain speed. Champion skateboard riders reach speeds up to 100 km per hour as they accelerate down steep inclines. Without friction, the champions could reach faster speeds, but they could not decelerate or stop!

Because of the Earth's gravity, skateboard riders may fall sometimes. Friction between the riders' bodies and the ground can cause cuts and bruises. Champion skateboard riders wear safety helmets, gloves, elbow and knee pads. These help to reduce injuries when riders fall.

Skateboarding is not as easy as it may look. It requires skillful control and balance. Champion skateboard riders have practiced for many years. They know how gravity and friction can be useful as well as harmful.

Chapter Review

Summary

- There are many kinds of forces that affect your world.
- Friction slows down moving objects.
- It would be impossible to move without friction.
- Friction causes the wearing away of surfaces.
- An electric force is the push or pull of electric charges.
- Every object has gravity that pulls on other objects.
- The force of gravity is affected by the distance between objects and the mass of objects.
- Pressure is a measure of the force on a certain area.
- Solids, liquids, and gases can apply pressure.

Science Words

friction   **electric force**   **pressure**
magnetic field   **gravity**

Questions

1. How are forces useful? How do they cause a problem?
2. How does friction slow down moving objects?
3. Think of a way magnetic forces can be measured.
4. How is the Earth's gravity measured?
5. Name two ways the pull of gravity between two objects can be changed.
6. If you put larger tires on a car, would you need more or less air pressure in them to support the car? Why?
7. You want to make a water gun shoot farther. Should you make the opening where the water comes out smaller or larger? Explain.
8. How can you decrease friction?
9. Sometimes when you comb your hair, a force causes some hairs to stand up. Name the force.
10. How do you use electric forces?

Chapter Three

Working with Forces

How do you know this girl is working? Why are forces important to her?

People use forces every day. We use many different forces in our lives. How are the people in these pictures using forces? What kinds of forces are they using? Why are the people using forces?

Work

All of the people in these pictures are using forces to do work. They are using a force to cause motion. Every time you kick a ball, open a door, or pedal a bike, you are using a force to cause motion. You may be having fun, but to a scientist you are doing work, too. In science, work has a special meaning. You are doing **work** when you use a force to cause motion.

187

When you lift an object, you use a force that pulls in a direction away from the Earth. If you lift a box, you are doing work. If you push the box across the floor, you are doing work.

Suppose your friend forgets his hat after school. He asks you to hold his books while he goes back for his hat. He offers to pay you for the time you spend doing work. When he returns, you ask for your money. He says he does not owe you any money because you have not done any work. According to the scientific meaning of work, you did not do any work! You used a force to hold the books, but you did not move them. If you use a force but cause no motion, you are not doing any work.

How Do We Measure Work?

We can measure the amount of work we do. To find out the amount of work, multiply the force times the distance the force moves an object. The newton-meter is the metric unit for work. **Joule** (JEWL) is another name for newton-meter and is a unit of work.

Suppose a force of one newton moves a book two meters. What is the amount of work done?

Work = Force × Distance Object Moved

Work = 1 newton × 2 meters

Work = 2 newton-meters or 2 joules

Activity

How Much Work Is Done When an Object Is Lifted?

What to use:

meter stick   string
objects to lift   pencil and paper
newton spring scale

What to do:

1. On your paper, make a chart like the one shown.

2. Attach an object to the spring scale. You may need to tie some objects with string.

3. Slowly lift or pull the object. Record how much force you used to lift or pull the object.

4. Ask a classmate to measure the distance you moved the object. Record the distance in meters.

5. Find out how much work you did by using:

Work = Force × Distance Object Moved

Record your answer on the chart.

6. Repeat steps 2 through 5 with other objects. Record your results on the chart.

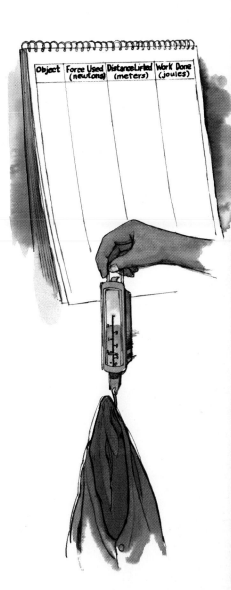

What did you learn?

1. What is the metric unit for work?
2. Which object did you work hardest to lift?
3. How did you find which one required the most work?

Using what you learned:

1. What are you measuring when you weigh an object with a newton spring scale?
2. How would the amount of work change if an object is moved twice, once at 11 meters and the second time at 22 meters?

1. When is work done?

2. A woman is lifting boxes. Each box requires a force of 120 newtons to move. She lifts 15 boxes from the ground onto the back of a truck. The back of the truck is half a meter off the ground. How much work did the woman do in lifting one box? 15 boxes?

How Do Machines Work?

The woman in one picture below is lifting boxes by hand. How would you know if she is doing work? You would get very tired if you had to lift heavy boxes all day. In the other picture below, the woman is using a machine to make her work

190

easier. Machines are devices that make work easier to do. Machines can increase a force or change the direction of a force. People may also use machines to do work more quickly. The machine the woman was using made lifting the boxes easier and she could lift them faster. People use many machines every day to do work. What machines did you use today to make your work easier or faster?

Some machines make work easier because they increase a force. The person in the picture below is using a machine to change a flat tire. Before she can change the tire, she must raise the front of the car off the ground. Alone, she does not have enough force to lift the car. The jack is a machine that increases the amount of force. The woman uses the jack to lift the car. The jack increases the force she can apply.

Machines can make work easier, but they require energy to do work. For many simple machines, a person is the source of energy. A person must use a force on the machine.

The amount that a machine can increase a force is called the **mechanical advantage** of the machine. Different machines can increase forces by different amounts. They have different mechanical advantages.

The mechanical advantage can be found for each machine. Divide the force of the machine by the force you used on the machine. Suppose the front of the car weighs 10,000 newtons. You must use a force of only 100 newtons on the jack. Find the mechanical advantage of the jack.

Mechanical advantage = 10,000 newtons
$\div$ 100 newtons

Mechanical advantage = 100

Suppose you are making a snow hut. You and your friend roll a large mound of snow for the side of the hut. Neither you nor your friend can move the heavy snow over to the hut. Your friend suggests using a lever to move it.

A lever is one type of machine. Imagine that you and your friend use a lever to move the snow mound which weighs 200 newtons. Together you use a force of 50 newtons on the lever. What is the mechanical advantage of using this machine to move the snow?

Some machines can be used to increase speed. It takes this boy twenty minutes to walk to school. He has to be there in fifteen minutes. You may think he will be late. He can get to school on time with a machine that increases his speed. What machine can he use?

Some machines make work easier by changing the direction of a force. The girl is pulling down, but the flag is going up. The girl is using a machine that changes the direction of her force.

Some complex machines use a fuel to produce the force. What is the energy source for the machine shown below?

Machines and Friction

You can measure how well machines do work by making two measurements. First, you must measure the amount of work that you have to put into the machine. Second, you must measure the amount of work done by the machine. The amount of work done by the machine will always be less than the amount of work you put into the machine. Friction reduces the amount of work the machine does. Friction changes some of the work you do into heat. The work that is changed into heat is wasted. Heat does not count as work done. The machine can do more work if there is less friction.

Friction is less when surfaces roll rather than slide over each other. Rolling friction is less than sliding friction. It is easier to push a chair on wheels than to slide a chair across the floor.

Activity

How Can You Make Less Friction?

What to use:
hand lens   3 marbles
liquid soap   pencil and paper

What to do:
1. Rub your hands together many times. Record what you feel.

2. Use the hand lens to look closely at your hands. Record what you see.

3. Put three marbles between your hands. Rub your hands together again. Record what you feel.

4. Put a little liquid soap in your hands. Rub them together again. Record what you feel.

What did you learn?
1. Describe the surfaces of your hands after each step.
2. Why did your hands feel different each time you rubbed them together?
3. What caused the difference?

Using what you learned:
1. How do marbles reduce friction?
2. How does the liquid soap reduce friction?
3. Why can you not get rid of all the friction?
4. How could you make more friction? Why would you want to make more friction?

A **bearing** is a round, smooth object you can put between two surfaces to reduce friction. The bearing causes rolling friction instead of sliding friction. The total amount of friction is reduced. In the picture, you can see bearings in the skate wheel. This type of bearing is called a ball bearing. Why do you think it got that name? The wheels of cars and bicycles also are like bearings. What other objects have bearings?

Another way to make less friction is to use lubricants. **Lubricants** (LEW brih kunts) are substances that make surfaces smooth and slippery. Smooth surfaces make less friction than rough surfaces. How could bearings and lubricants be used to make less friction in machines? You may use oil as a lubricant on your bike. Where have you seen other lubricants and bearings in machines?

Think of the machines you have in your home. How do they reduce your work? What lubricants or bearings do machines use to reduce friction?

Chapter Review

Summary

- Work is done when a force moves an object.
- Joule or a newton-meter is the unit used to measure work.
- Machines make work easier by increasing the force or by changing the direction of a force.
- Mechanical advantage measures how much a machine increases a force.
- Bearings and lubricants reduce friction in machines.

Science Words

work   **mechanical advantage**   **lubricants**
joule   **bearing**

Questions

1. What happens when work is done?
2. How much work is done if a person uses 50 newtons of force to move a desk two meters?
3. How do bearings and lubricants reduce friction in machines?
4. Why do people use machines?
5. A person exerts a force of 30 newtons on a machine. An object is moved by the machine, requiring 90 newtons. What is the mechanical advantage of the machine?
6. A person uses a machine to lift a 25-newton box. The mechanical advantage of the machine is 5. What force must the person use on the machine?
7. Which of the following are examples of doing work?
   (a) shoveling snow
   (b) holding up a heavy table while someone fixes one leg
8. After riding your bike with the brakes on, you touch the brake pads. How do they feel? Why?

Unit 5 Review

 Self Checks

Answer these Self Checks on a sheet of paper.

1. Define position and motion.
2. What causes objects to move?
3. What is the speed of a person who walks 20 kilometers in five hours?
4. Give an example of acceleration and an example of deceleration.
5. Give two examples of forces. Tell why they are important to you.
6. Give an example where work is being done and an example where no work is being done.
7. A force of 15 newtons is used on a machine in order to lift a 30-newton object a distance of 2 meters.
   (a) How much work is done by the machine?
   (b) What is the mechanical advantage of the machine?
8. Tell how these machines help people do work.

a

b

c

Idea Corner
More Fun with Science

1. Find your speed when you walk to school. You will need to know:

   (a) the distance from your house to your school.

   (b) how long it takes you to walk to school.

2. Talk with someone who repairs machines. Ask how friction is reduced in the machines and report what you learn.

3. Find out how magnets are used in electric motors. Report your findings to the class.

4. Using the spring from a mousetrap, build a "mousetrap car." CAUTION: Be careful when using the spring. Have a contest to find out who can build a car that will go the farthest. How does friction affect your car?

5. Find out how much work you do walking up stairs. You will need to know the distance of the stairs in meters from the bottom step to the top step and your weight in newtons.

Reading for Fun

Bet You Can't! Science Impossibilities to Fool You by Vicki Cobb and Kathy Darling, Lathrop, Lee and Shepard Books: New York, © 1980.

   Keep your friends entertained for hours.

Let's Play Science by Mary Stetten, Harper Colophon Books: New York, © 1979.

   Learn many ideas for science projects and fun.

Up, Up and Away! The Story of Ballooning by Anabel Dean, Westminster Company: New York, © 1980.

   This history of ballooning discusses scientific concepts.

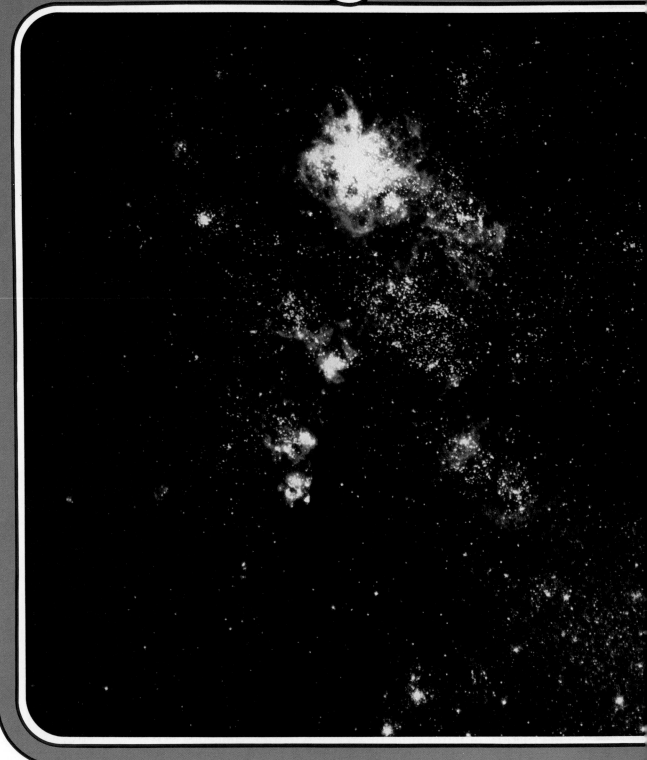

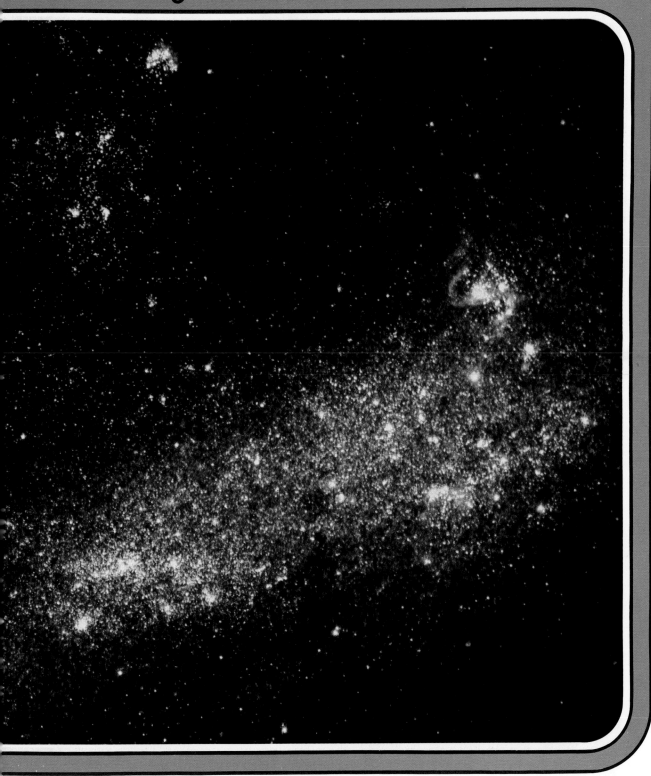

Chapter One
Stars and Galaxies

How many stars can you see at night? What differences can you see in the stars? What do scientists know about the stars?

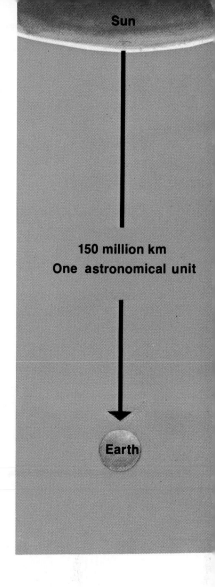

Sun

150 million km
One astronomical unit

Earth

Many people enjoy observing the stars at night. Stargazing usually raises some questions. People may want to know how many stars there are or how far away they are. What questions do you have about the stars?

The stars in the night sky do not appear the same to all observers. City lights block out the light from many stars. From different parts of the Earth, people see different stars. Telescopes also help people see more stars.

Distances in Space

Astronomers (uh STRAHN uh murz) are scientists who study the stars. Astronomers try to find answers to questions about the stars. Astronomers study the sun to learn more about other stars.

The sun is the star closest to the Earth. The distance from the Earth to the sun is called one **astronomical** (as truh NAHM ih kul) **unit.** One astronomical unit is about 150,000,000 kilometers.

Astronomers use astronomical units to measure distances in our solar system. Yet, the astronomical unit is too short to use for distances to most stars. It would be like measuring the distance from your home to your school with a piece of string one centimeter long. Why would measuring this way be difficult?

Astronomers use light-years to talk about distances in space. A **light-year** is the distance light travels in one year. Light travels fast. The distance light travels in a year is very far.

Other than the sun, Alpha Centauri (AL fuh·sen TAWR ee) is one of the closest stars to Earth. The distance to Alpha Centauri is over four light-years. It takes light from this star over four years to reach the Earth. Compare four years to eight minutes which is the time it takes the light from our sun to reach the Earth. Other stars are hundreds of light-years from the Earth. Some are even thousands of light-years away!

Activity

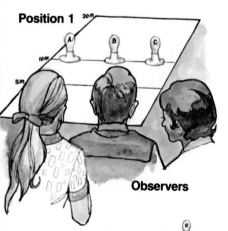

Position 1

Observers

Position 2

Observers

What Affects the Brightness of an Object?

What to use:

3 extension cords
3 lamps: A—with 40-watt bulb
        B—with 75-watt bulb
        C—with 100-watt bulb

tape measure
observers
pencil and paper

What to do:

1. Make the room as dark as possible. Turn on all lamps at a distance of 10 m from the observers. Call this position 1. Observe the brightest lamp. Record your observation.

2. Move lamp B to a distance of 5 m from the observers. Move lamp C to a distance of 20 m from the observers. Do not move lamp A. Call this position 2. Observe the brightest lamp. Record your observation.

What did you learn?

1. Which lamp appeared the brightest in position 1? Which lamp is giving off the most light?
2. Which lamp appeared the brightest in position 2? Which lamp is giving off the most light?

Using what you learned:

1. Which lamp, in brightness, is most like our sun?
2. Why does our sun appear so bright when compared to the size and distance of other stars?

Brightness

Some stars that appear brighter than others actually may not be so bright. Pretend you are observing two stars that are both the same distance from the Earth. Both appear to be the same brightness. Now suppose one star were twice as far away as the other. Which would look brighter? Distances in space make some very bright stars appear dim. Distances can also make some dim stars appear very bright.

Ancient observers thought all stars were the same distance from the Earth. They thought all dim stars were small and all bright stars were big. Today, astronomers think our sun is an average-sized star compared to the other stars. Why does it appear to be the brightest star?

Making Sure

1. How long is one astronomical unit?
2. What is a light-year?
3. What factors affect how bright a star appears?

Star Sizes

Astronomers know stars are not all the same size. Our sun is over one million times bigger in volume than the Earth. Some stars are smaller than our sun. Others are much larger. Very small stars are called **dwarf stars.** Some dwarf stars are no larger than the Earth.

There are many stars larger than our sun. The largest stars are called **giant stars.** Antares (an TAR eez) is a giant star. About three million stars the size of our sun could fit into Antares.

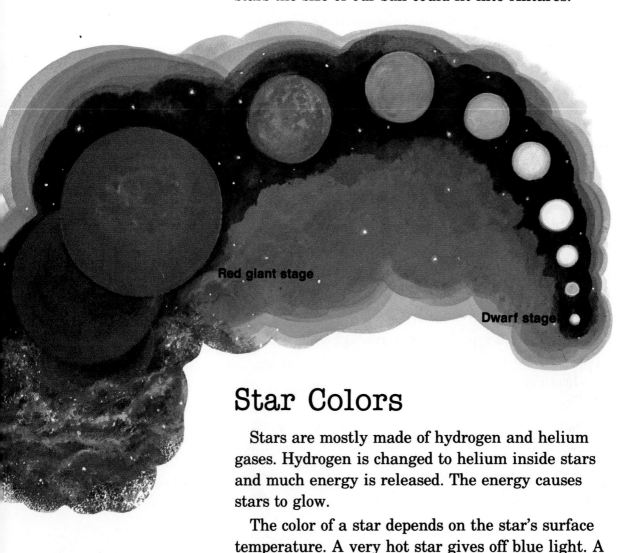

Red giant stage

Dwarf stage

Star Colors

Stars are mostly made of hydrogen and helium gases. Hydrogen is changed to helium inside stars and much energy is released. The energy causes stars to glow.

The color of a star depends on the star's surface temperature. A very hot star gives off blue light. A cooler star, like Antares, is red. Our sun is yellow.

Look at the chart below. What is the surface temperature of our sun? How does the surface temperature of our sun differ from the surface temperature of Antares?

Star Colors and Surface Temperatures				
Color	Red	Yellow	White	Blue
Temperature	3000°C	6000°C	7000°C	21,000°C

Milky Way Galaxy

Imagine taking a ride in space on a beam of light from the sun. In just eight minutes, you would arrive at Earth. You would reach Saturn and its rings in about one hour and 15 minutes. After five hours and 10 minutes, you would pass Pluto. Soon you would be out of the solar system. Traveling at the speed of light, it would take years to reach the closest star to the sun.

As you travel from star to star, you would be traveling in a galaxy. A **galaxy** is a large group of stars, gas, and dust. It is made of billions of stars.

Our sun

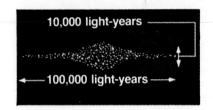

10,000 light-years

100,000 light-years

There are large distances between the stars. Our sun and the planets in our solar system are part of a galaxy called the Milky Way. Astronomers believe that the Milky Way is shaped like a saucer with a thick center and thin edges. The thickness of the center is about 10,000 light-years. Moving at the speed of light, how long would it take you to travel through the center of the Milky Way? The distance across the Milky Way galaxy is about 100,000 light-years.

Our sun is only one star in the galaxy. Most of the stars we see in the sky are part of our galaxy. On a clear night, you can see the stars along the flat, saucer-shaped part of our galaxy. They look like a milky white path. The sky looks that way because we are inside the galaxy looking through it.

Other Galaxies

Using telescopes, astronomers have found other galaxies. Some of these galaxies are star groups like our Milky Way. Some galaxies are so far away that their energy can be found only by special telescopes.

Astronomers notice that galaxies seem to be in groups. Our galaxy is part of a group called the Local Group. The term local is used because the galaxies in that group are close to each other. Astronomers know of at least twenty members in the Local Group.

You might compare a galaxy to a town or city. Galaxy groups would be like a number of towns or cities that are not far apart. Farther away might be another cluster or group of towns, or another galaxy group. There are many galaxy groups spread out through space. All of these galaxies and the space around them make up the universe. Astronomers do not know whether there is an end to the stars. They

Small Cloud of Magellan

keep discovering more and more stars, farther and farther away. What number of stars do you think there are?

Astronomers have photographed many members of our Local Group. The closest galaxies to the Milky Way are the Clouds of Magellan. There are two of these cloud-shaped galaxies. They are called the Large and Small Clouds of Magellan. Each of these is smaller than the Milky Way. They also have very different shapes from the Milky Way. They are both about 200,000 light-years from the center of the Milky Way.

The Clouds of Magellan can be seen without a telescope. The explorer Magellan observed these galaxies in the night sky on one of his voyages. They are seen only from the Southern Hemisphere.

Another galaxy in the Local Group is Andromeda (an DRAHM ud uh). Some astronomers call Andromeda our twin galaxy. It is about the same size and shape as the Milky Way galaxy. Andromeda is over 2,000,000 light-years from our galaxy. On a very clear, dark night, away from the city lights, you can see Andromeda. It looks like a fuzzy patch of light. Andromeda is the galaxy shown here. The Andromeda galaxy and the Clouds of Magellan are the only galaxies seen without a telescope.

Andromeda galaxy

Types of Galaxies

Galaxies are different in size and shape. Different types of galaxies are named for their shape. They are irregular, spiral, or elliptical (ih LIHP tih kul).

Galaxies that do not have any special shape or form are called **irregular galaxies.** There is no star pattern in irregular galaxies. They can have many different shapes. The two Clouds of Magellan are irregular galaxies. Irregular galaxies are not very common.

Spiral galaxies have spiral or curved arms. The arms curve around the center of the galaxies. Spiral galaxies have definite star patterns. The Milky Way and Andromeda are spiral galaxies. Some spiral galaxies have a slightly different shape than the Milky Way and Andromeda galaxies.

Elliptical galaxies are shaped like an oval with a definite pattern of stars. Some think they look like spiral galaxies without arms. Many individual stars can be seen around their edges. Depending upon how you look at them, elliptical galaxies have different shapes. Sometimes elliptical galaxies look round to us. How can an egg-shaped object look round? Other elliptical galaxies look like pancakes.

Astronomers have learned many things about the stars. There is still much more to learn. As old questions are answered, new questions arise.

Irregular galaxy   Spiral galaxy   Elliptical galaxy

People and Science

Following the Stars

Where are you now? Where are you going? It is easy to answer these questions when you are on land. Imagine being in the middle of an ocean! Everywhere you look you see water. How would you know where you are or where you are going? A ship's navigator (NAV uh gay tuhr) must know how to find locations at sea.

Near the shore the navigator observes lighthouses and landmarks. It is not difficult to know the ship's location. At sea, the navigator finds location and direction by observing the sun and other stars. Just after sunset and before sunrise each day

the navigator observes the sky. He looks for familiar stars, such as Betelgeuse (BEE tuhl joos) in the constellation Orion. The navigator uses a sextant to observe several stars. With a sextant he measures the direction of the stars and their angles above the horizon.

This information helps the navigator find the ship's location on maps or charts of the sea. The navigator keeps a daily record of the ship's locations. He tells the ship's captain how to get from one land to another. When the ship reaches land again, the ship's navigator knows he has done his job well.

Chapter Review

Summary

- An astronomical unit is the distance from the Earth to the sun.
- A light-year is the distance light travels in one year.
- Not all stars are the same size.
- Stars are different in brightness because of distance and size.
- A star's color depends on its surface temperature.
- Galaxies are large groups of stars, gas, and dust.
- Our solar system is in the Milky Way galaxy.
- Galaxies are classified irregular, spiral, and elliptical because of their shape.

Science Words

astronomers	dwarf stars	irregular galaxies
astronomical unit	giant stars	spiral galaxies
light-year	galaxy	elliptical galaxies

Questions

1. How is an astronomical unit like a light-year?
2. How are a light-year and an astronomical unit different?
3. What unit is used to measure distances to planets? Why?
4. Why do some smaller stars look brighter than some larger stars?
5. How could a dwarf star look brighter than a giant star?
6. Which is hotter, a yellow star or a blue star?
7. Since our sun is yellow, what is its temperature?
8. Describe the shape of the Milky Way galaxy.
9. In what galaxy is Alpha Centauri?
10. How are the Clouds of Magellan and Andromeda alike?
11. How are galaxies grouped or classified?
12. What type of galaxy is Andromeda?

Chapter Two
Patterns in the Sky

How would you describe the arrangement of these stars? What patterns can you see? What other star patterns do you know?

Night sky in the country

Gaze at the sky on a clear night. If you live in the city or near a lot of lights, you may not be able to see many stars. The lights may block out some of the stars. Still, you will see the brightest stars.

At first glance, the stars appear scattered all over the sky. If you look carefully, you may see certain groups or patterns of stars. People of long ago saw patterns in the stars. They imagined lines connecting the stars. These pictures were like the connect-the-dots games you may have played. When the stars were connected by imaginary lines, the people could see a picture or constellation.

Night sky in the city

Constellations

A star group with a definite pattern is called a **constellation** (kahn stuh LAY shun). Each constellation has a different pattern. Some constellations have many stars. Others have only a few. Each constellation is found in a special place in the sky.

Activity

What Star Pattern Can You Make?

What to use:

10 gummed stars   white crayon
blue or black paper   paper and pencil

What to do:

1. Hold the gummed stars above the paper. Drop them. Paste the stars where they land.

2. Use your imagination to "see" a person, animal, or object in this star group.

3. Draw lines between the stars with the white crayon to make the pattern you imagined. Give it a name.

What did you learn?

1. What did you imagine?
2. What patterns did you make with the stars and crayon lines?

Using what you learned:

1. Ancient people connected one group of stars like this drawing. What would you name this pattern?
2. Use your book and other books to find some constellations. Trace the star patterns on a separate piece of paper. Connect the stars in each pattern. What do they look like to you?

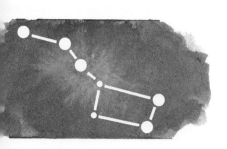

Long ago people spent a lot of time looking at star patterns. They used the stars to find north, south, east, and west at night. Travelers on land and on water followed certain bright stars and constellations. During the night, the stars seemed to travel across the sky. They appeared to move from east to west. Stars above the poles seemed to move in circles.

Stars and constellations were very important to people long ago. These people used the night sky to tell time. The movement of stars showed the time of night just as the movement of the sun showed the time of day. The phases of the moon showed the time of the month. The appearance and motion of constellations marked the seasons of the year. Crop planting, festivals, and other events were planned according to the movement of the stars. Today people still plan some of their activities by star movements.

People long ago named the star patterns for objects, animals, or famous people they knew. The names of the constellations described what people thought the star patterns looked like. Sometimes it is hard for us to imagine how people saw such pictures. The stars in a pattern provided only part of the picture. Their imaginations supplied the rest of the picture. People made up stories or legends to go with the constellations.

Yearly Patterns

One famous star pattern that looks like its name is the **Big Dipper.** There are seven stars in the Big Dipper. Four stars make the bowl of the dipper. Three stars form the handle. Notice the two brightest stars on the end of the bowl in the Big Dipper. These are called the Pointer Stars. The Pointer Stars form a line pointing to the North Star.

Polaris (puh LER us) is called the North Star. **Polaris** is the star located above the Earth's north pole. People have used Polaris to find directions. If they were lost, Polaris showed where north was. Polaris was known to the American Indians as the "star that does not move." By knowing which direction was north, they were able to find south, east, and west. If you were outside facing north, east is to your right. Where is west? Where is southeast?

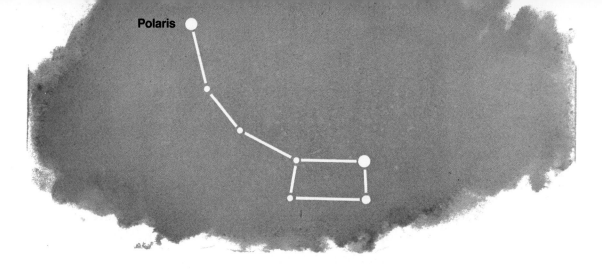

Polaris

Polaris is the last and brightest star in the handle of the Little Dipper. The **Little Dipper** is a star pattern that looks like a smaller Big Dipper. The Little Dipper has a bowl of four stars and a handle of three stars. How many stars are there in the Big Dipper? The Little Dipper is not visible in the night sky when there are a lot of lights. It must be very dark before many stars can be seen. What does the name of this pattern suggest about its size compared to the Big Dipper? In what direction would you find the Little Dipper?

Polaris and the Big Dipper can be used to find other star patterns. The constellation Cassiopeia (kas ee uh PEE uh) is one of these. It seems to circle Polaris all year. Cassiopeia and the Big Dipper are opposite each other with Polaris between them.

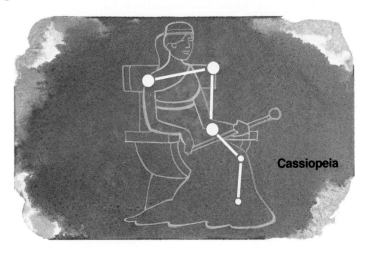

Cassiopeia

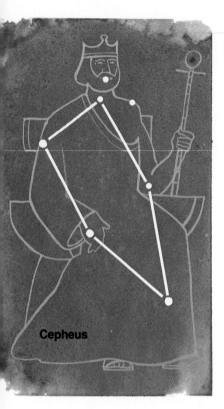

Cepheus

Cassiopeia is shaped like the letter M or W. Early Greek people thought this star pattern looked like a queen sitting on her throne. It may be hard for you to imagine a queen from just five stars, but people long ago did.

Near the queen, the Greeks saw a king. They named him Cepheus (SEE fee us). One end of Cepheus is about halfway between Polaris and Cassiopeia. It is a large constellation that looks like a square and a triangle. Some think it looks like a doghouse. How would you describe its shape?

All these constellations seem to circle or revolve around Polaris during the year. Each constellation appears to change its position as the seasons change. For example, you might see Cassiopeia as a W in the winter and an M in summer. Even the Dippers appear upside down in certain times of the year. How might you describe the position of Cepheus during the year?

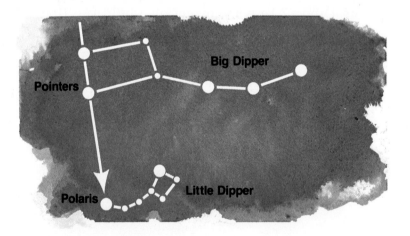

Big Dipper

Pointers

Polaris

Little Dipper

Making Sure

1. What is a constellation?
2. Why is the Earth's pole star important for locating other stars and constellations?

This star chart shows each of the constellations near Polaris. If you live north of the equator, you can see these constellations throughout the year. Rotate the page so the winter months are at the top. The stars are shown as they would appear in the early evening winter sky. Do the same for spring, summer, and fall.

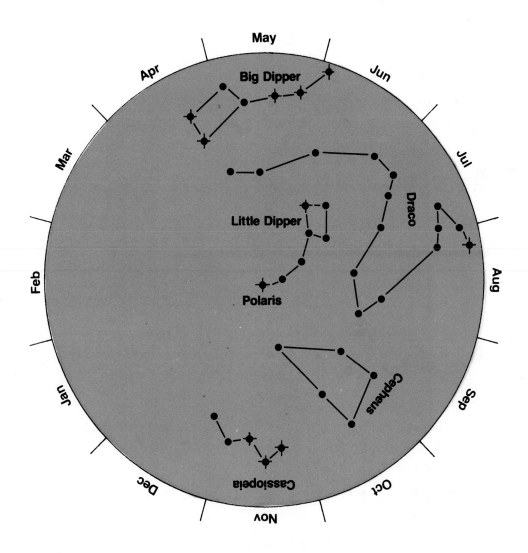

In which direction do these constellations move around Polaris? How would you describe the position of Polaris?

Constellations of the Seasons

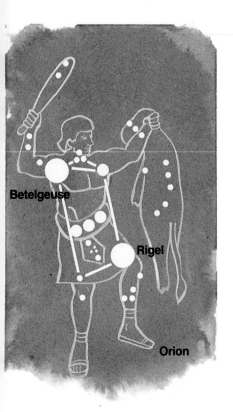

Imagine a hunter in the sky as the early Greeks did. They saw Orion, the mighty hunter, in the star patterns. You can see Orion best during the winter months. Orion is a very large constellation. The two brightest stars in Orion are located at his right shoulder and left knee. Three other bright stars form the hunter's belt. You may be able to imagine a sword hanging from the belt.

Many hunters have dogs. Orion's constellation dog, Canis Major, is found near Orion's right heel. As you view Orion in the sky, Canis Major is on the left of Orion. The dog constellation includes **Sirius** (SIHR ee us), the brightest star in the night sky. You can use Orion's belt stars as pointers to find Sirius. The line made by the belt stars points south to Sirius.

Another constellation best seen in winter is Taurus. The early Greeks imagined the stars in the

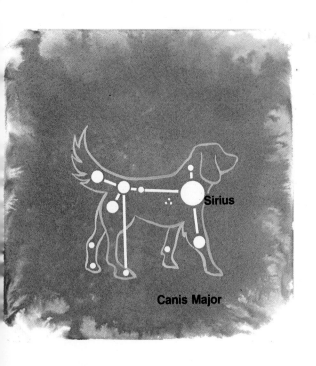

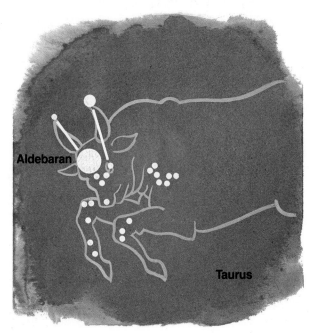

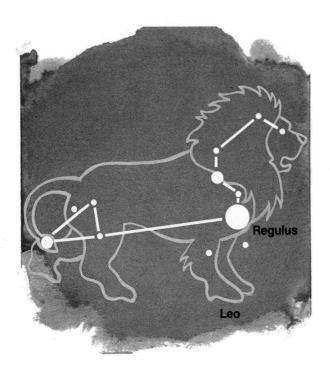

Leo

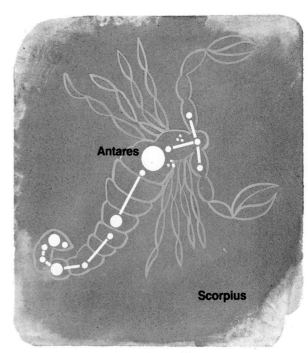

Antares

Scorpius

shape of the letter V. The V formed the head of a bull. Taurus is just west of Orion. Orion seems to be chasing Taurus, the bull, through the winter sky.

Leo the Lion is a very famous constellation in the spring sky. Leo is in the southern part of the sky during March, April, and May. Look for a backward question mark and a triangle. You can also find Leo by using the pointer stars of the Big Dipper. Looking north, the pointer stars point to Polaris. Looking south, the pointer stars point to Leo.

The summer night sky offers some unusual star patterns. In early summer, there is the fishhook-shaped star pattern, Scorpius. The Greeks imagined the curved row of stars to be a scorpion's tail. They also imagined Scorpius was a dangerous animal for Orion. Scorpius was the only animal Orion could not kill.

Fall ends with the appearance of the constellation Auriga (aw RI guh) in the northeast sky. Auriga, the chariot driver, is close to Taurus, the bull.

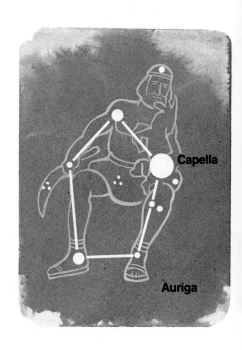

Capella

Auriga

How Can You Make a Constellation Model?

What to use:

tin can (both ends open)
2 pieces black construction paper
3 nails of different widths

clear tape
scissors
pencil and paper

What to do:

1. CAUTION: Be sure the can has no rough edges. Use black construction paper and tape to line the inside of the can.

2. Trace and cut the outline of the can end on another piece of black construction paper. Leave the tabs.

3. Find a picture of your favorite constellation and copy it on the paper circle. Using the nails, punch small holes in the paper circle to mark each star.

4. Turn the star pattern circle over and tape it on one can end. Tape it so no light comes into the can.

5. Hold the can up to the light and look through it from the open end. CAUTION: Do not look at the sun as it may cause blindness.

What did you learn?

1. Why do you think the inside of the can was lined with black paper?
2. How might people use constellation models?

Using what you learned:

1. Read and write stories about your constellation.
2. What constellations appear in spring in your area?

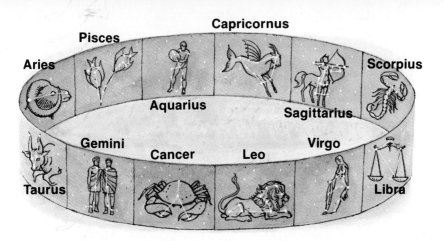

Twelve Special Constellations

People long ago observed that the sun follows the same path across the sky every year. They called the path of the sun the **zodiac.** Zodiac is a Greek word that means "wheel of life." The zodiac is divided into twelve sections. Each section contains a constellation. The constellations are called the twelve signs of the zodiac. The signs are named after people, animals, and one object.

You cannot see all the constellations of the zodiac at one time. The signs change with the seasons. This change is caused by the movement of the Earth around the sun. Each zodiac sign is seen best during a certain time of the year.

The zodiac was used as a calendar by people long ago. The sun always appeared to travel along the zodiac. People watched to see near which constellation the sun appeared to rise and set. If the sun's path traveled near Taurus, they knew it was early spring. If the sun traveled along Virgo's path, they knew it was late summer.

The constellations offer an exciting way to watch the night sky. Each season brings a new display of stars. Which constellations are your favorites? In which season is your very favorite constellation seen most easily?

Sky Calendars

There are millions of stones arranged in circles on the Great Plains of North America. The stones are about the size of loaves of bread. The circles vary in size. Some of the largest circles are nearly 25 meters across. These large circles are called medicine wheels. They look like wheels with spokes.

No one knows who built the medicine wheels. Scientists wondered why many of the wheels have 28 spokes. Since there are 28 days in a "moon" or an Indian month, the scientists thought the medicine wheels may have been sky calendars.

Scientists studied the medicine wheels. From different viewing places on the circles, they found that the stones pointed to the sun and to certain stars. In fact, the stones of the medicine wheels seemed to be marking a certain day of the year— the summer solstice (SUHL stis). The summer solstice is the first day of summer. On this day every year the sun is highest in the sky.

The Indians of the Great Plains had many ceremonies in the summer. The most important ceremony was the sun dance. Today many people believe the Plains Indians did use the medicine wheels as calendars. The sky calendars may have been used to mark the dates of the sun dance and other events throughout the year.

Chapter Review

Summary

- Constellations are star groups with a certain pattern.
- People of long ago named constellations after familiar objects, animals, and people.
- The appearance and motion of constellations marked the seasons of the year for people of long ago.
- Polaris, the North Star, does not change position.
- Constellations near Polaris can be seen all year.
- Some constellations are most easily seen during one season of the year.
- Sirius, the brightest star in the sky, is seen near the constellation Orion.
- Twelve special constellations appear along a path called the zodiac.

Science Words

constellation   **Polaris**   **Sirius**
Big Dipper   **Little Dipper**   **zodiac**

Questions

1. What name is given to groups of stars that make a pattern?
2. In what direction do the stars appear to move each night?
3. How did people of long ago use constellations?
4. How would you find Polaris?
5. Why did the Indians call Polaris the "star that does not move"?
6. How could Polaris be useful to you if you were lost?
7. What constellations can be seen all year?
8. If you saw Sirius, what season would it be?
9. What season is best for observing the chariot driver?
10. Why was the zodiac important to ancient people?

Self Checks

Answer these Self Checks on a sheet of paper.

1. What causes stars to look bright or dim?
2. How are constellations and galaxies alike? How are they different?
3. What is the shape of the Milky Way galaxy?
4. Name each of the constellations here. What time of the year can you see them?

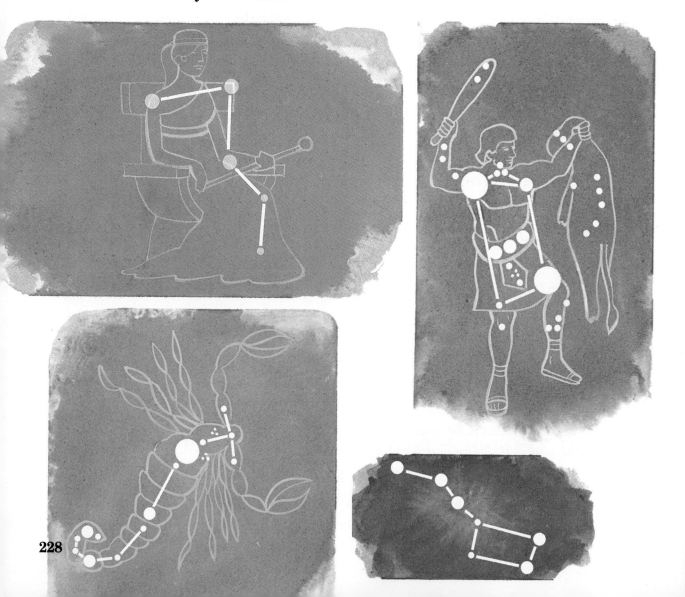

228

💡 Idea Corner
More Fun with Science

1. Observe the movement of a constellation over several hours. Draw the constellation at various times to show its movement.

2. Use an overhead or slide projector to show models of several constellations. Give hints such as the time of year each is found in the night sky.

3. Use library resources to find out about the Crab Nebula and the Horsehead Nebula. Find some pictures or drawings and show them to your class.

4. Read about the legends of the American Indians and the star patterns they viewed. Give a report to your class.

5. Design a new constellation and write a story or myth about it. Display the constellation and give a report to your class.

Reading for Fun

Eavesdropping on Space: The Quest of Radio Astronomy by David Knight, William Morrow and Company: New York, © 1975.

Read about the search for new matter in space.

The Heavenly Zoo: Legends and Tales of the Stars by Lurie Alison, Farrar Books: New York, © 1980.

Find out about additional legends and stories of the constellations.

The Night Sky Book: An Everyday Guide to Every Night by Jamie Jobb, Little, Brown and Company: Boston, © 1977.

Games, projects, and charts will help you find the constellations in the night sky.

Unit 7

Energy Around Us

Chapter One
Types of Energy

What is energy? Where do you get energy? How have you used energy today?

You may know people who have a lot of energy. You may hear on the radio and TV and read in newspapers about a shortage of energy. Sometimes when you are tired or hungry, you may say you need some energy. What are you really talking about when you say "energy"?

What Is Energy?

What does energy look like? You have never seen energy. Yet, you can see what energy does. Think of people who have a lot of energy. What do these people do? They can move rapidly or do a lot of work.

For example, look at the girls in the picture. They are climbing to the top of the ropes as quickly as they can. It takes energy to do that work. You cannot see the energy they are using. Instead, you see the results of their energy. You see them climb to the top of the rope. You can see the work done by the girls.

Energy is the ability to do work. Remember, we have a special meaning for work. Work is done only when a force is used to move an object. You need energy to do the work. What work is being done by the girl in the picture? What work have you done?

Different Types of Energy

There are different types of energy. Imagine you are riding a bicycle. What work are you doing? Work is done because you are moved by the force you are exerting on the pedals of the bicycle. The energy of any object in motion is called **kinetic** (kuh NET ihk) **energy.** Since you are in motion, you have kinetic energy. Any moving matter has kinetic energy. What objects do you see that have kinetic energy?

234

Objects that are not in motion can also have energy. A car stopped at the top of a hill has energy. It does not have kinetic energy because it is not in motion. Yet, it has the ability to do work. This type of energy is called potential (puh TEN chul) energy. **Potential energy** is energy that is stored. For example, the stopped car has potential energy because of its position on the top of the hill. Gravity can help cause the car roll down the hill. Another example of potential energy is a stretched rubber band. Because of its stretched position, it has potential energy. If you let go of the stretched rubber band, it will move. How could the rubber band be given more potential energy?

Potential energy can change to kinetic energy. As a car goes down the hill, the energy changes. The energy is no longer stored or potential energy. Since the car is in motion, the potential energy changes to kinetic energy.

Activity

How Do Potential and Kinetic Energy Differ?

What to use:

ball (tennis or Ping-Pong)
paper, 120 cm long   meter stick
tape   graph paper
felt marker   pencil and paper

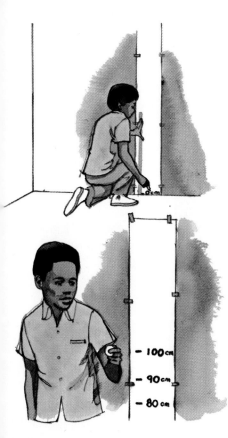

What to do:

1. Work with a partner to tape the long paper to a wall as shown. Be sure the bottom edge of the paper touches the floor.

2. Measure and mark the paper with the meter stick and felt marker. Mark zero at the bottom edge of the paper. Measure and mark every 10 cm up to 100 cm.

3. Hold the ball at the 100-cm mark but away from the wall. Drop the ball and let it bounce twice. Have your partner note and record how high it bounces each time. Mark the two bounce heights on the paper with a pencil.

4. Drop the ball from other heights and mark the bounce heights. Make a graph to show the height of drop and the height of bounce.

What did you learn?

1. At what height of the bounce does the ball have the greatest potential energy? At what height does the ball have the greatest kinetic energy?

2. At what height does the potential energy of the ball begin to change to kinetic energy?

3. At what height is the kinetic energy of the ball being changed back to potential energy?

1. On a separate piece of paper, list the letters of each picture in order of the most potential energy to least potential energy. Then list the pictures in order of the least kinetic energy to the most kinetic energy.
2. What do you notice about the order of each list?

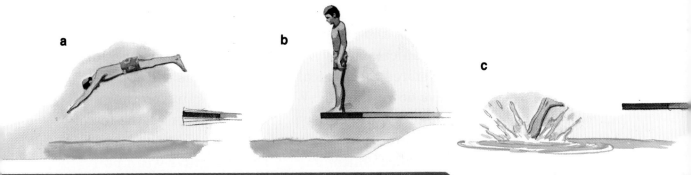

a
b
c

Forms of Kinetic and Potential Energy

When you think of a person with a lot of energy, you may think of someone who moves a lot. The motion of that person is mechanical energy. **Mechanical energy** is energy due to the motion or position of people or objects. Moving people and objects have mechanical energy.

People and objects that are not moving have stored mechanical energy. A skier standing on top of a hill has stored mechanical energy. She has the ability to move down the hill. What force is acting on the skier? Because of her position, the skier on the top of the hill has potential energy. Any object can have stored mechanical energy because gravity can pull on any object. Cars on a hill have mechanical energy. Look at the girls below. One is higher than the other. Which girl has more stored mechanical energy? A wound alarm clock has stored mechanical energy, also.

Chemical (KEM ih kul) energy is a form of potential energy. **Chemical energy** is energy stored in molecules of matter. Chemical energy is stored energy that is given off when some molecules of matter react with each other. A battery is one example of stored chemical energy. Wood to be burned has stored chemical energy.

People often talk about a shortage of energy. Usually, they mean a shortage of fuel. Fuel has stored chemical energy. Chemical energy is very important to us. Most of our chemical energy is used to make heat. **Heat energy** is the movement of the particles that make up a substance. Since particles in a substance move, what type of energy is heat energy? Food has stored chemical energy. Chemical energy in food is changed to heat or mechanical energy. Your body uses heat energy to remain warm. Mechanical energy is any movement your body makes. Why does your body need chemical energy?

Calories in Foods			
Apple	90	Margarine	100
Banana	110	Milk, 1 glass	160
Carrots, 1 cup	40	Orange juice	90
Cookie, sugar	35	Potato, baked	145
Dry cereal	60	Sausage, 1 serving	500
Hamburger	200	Toast, 1 slice	80
Hamburger bun	120		

Calories the Body Uses per Hour	
Sitting	48
Writing	64
Walking	160
Going down stairs	180
Exercising	200
Running	300
Going up stairs	560

Sometimes people eat more food than they need. They take in more energy than they use. The body's extra energy is stored as fat. The stored energy in food is measured in units called Calories. One chart above lists the Calories found in some foods. How many Calories have you consumed today? The other chart shows how many Calories of energy are needed to do some activities. How many Calories would it take for you to walk for 30 minutes? About how many Calories of energy would you need during a 15-minute recess period? Find out how many Calories your body needs each day.

Electric energy is energy due to the charged particles of matter. Current electricity is the flow of charged particles through paths or circuits. Current electricity is used to run machines or light rooms. Current electricity has both kinetic and potential energy. It has only potential energy when there is not a flow of electric particles.

Making Sure

1. What is the difference between kinetic and potential energy?
2. Is the energy in an orange kinetic or potential?

Radiant energy is a form of energy that travels in waves. Radiant energy can be transferred between objects separated by empty space. **Light energy** is visible radiant energy. Light energy can travel from the sun to the Earth through space. It can also travel through some matter. Light energy from a lamp or flashlight travels through the air. Through what other matter can light energy travel? Through what matter can light energy not travel?

Solar energy is radiant energy from the sun. Solar energy must travel through space to reach Earth. Solar energy is the most important energy for Earth. Plants would not grow without light from solar energy. What would happen to people and other animals without plants? Some people use solar energy to heat their homes and run some machines. It can be used to cook food. In what ways have you heard about or seen people using solar energy?

Solar home

X rays are also radiant energy. X rays are invisible. They can travel through gases, liquids, and some solids. You may have seen X-ray pictures of your teeth. X rays can travel through your skin, but they are absorbed and reflected by your teeth and bones. In this way, pictures of your teeth and bones can be taken. What part of the body is shown in this X-ray picture?

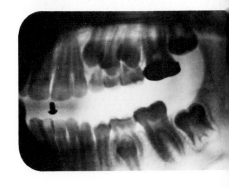

Radio waves are radiant energy, too. Radio waves can travel through gases but bounce off solids and some liquids. The reflected waves behave like echoes. These **reflected** waves can be used to locate objects or precipitation. **Radar** is a method used to locate objects or precipitation using radio waves.

Weather forecasters use radar. At many weather stations, radio waves are sent out. The radio waves are reflected by precipitation in the air. The reflected radio waves are seen on a special radar screen. The forecasters can locate where the precipitation is and the direction it is moving. This allows forecasters to warn people who may need to take cover when a severe storm is coming.

Radar is used by air controllers to control air traffic. Radio waves are sent out. When the waves strike an airplane, they bounce back and controllers can see each airplane on the radar screen. The crowded air around big airports is much safer because of radar. Radar is useful on ships, also. In what ways would a ship find radar useful?

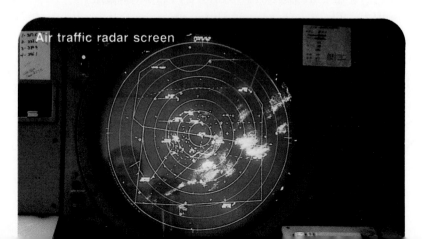

Air traffic radar screen

Chapter Review

Summary

- Energy is the ability to do work.
- Energy of motion is called kinetic energy.
- Stored energy is called potential energy.
- Mechanical energy is energy due to the motion or position of people and objects.
- Chemical energy is energy stored in molecules of matter.
- Heat energy is the movement of the particles of a substance.
- Electric energy is the energy of charged particles of matter.
- Radiant energy includes light energy, solar energy, X rays, and radio waves.

Science Words

energy	chemical energy	light energy
kinetic energy	heat energy	solar energy
potential energy	electric energy	X rays
mechanical energy	radiant energy	radar

Questions

1. What is the difference between potential and kinetic energy?
2. What does radiant energy include?
3. Name some forms of energy which you used today.
4. Tell whether these examples indicate mechanical, chemical, heat, electric, radiant, light, or solar energy.
   (a) a campfire
   (b) the sun
   (c) a diver ready to dive into water
   (d) a car going down the street
5. Name three examples of potential energy.
6. What happens if you eat more chemical energy than you need?

Chapter Two
Chains of Energy

What is energy? How do we get energy from one place to another? How does energy change from one form to another?

Suppose you are at a soccer game. It is almost over. The score is four to three, and your team is losing by one point. One of the players kicks the ball right into the goal box. Your team has scored a point! The game is tied four to four now.

The ball moves back and forth between each team several times. Yet no points are scored. One player uses his knee to bounce the ball to another team member. The second player kicks the ball across the field to a third player. The third player kicks the ball into the goal box with great force. A point is scored. Your team wins!

Energy Sources and Receivers

It takes a great deal of energy to play a soccer game. Many objects must be moved fast. Since forces are used to move objects, we know work is done during a soccer game. A lot of energy is needed. From where did the energy come? Where did the energy go?

You know that each player has energy. We can call each player an energy source. An **energy source** is a person or object that gives off energy. Energy from an energy source moves to another person or object. The person or object receiving the energy is called an **energy receiver.**

Think about the players who helped make the winning point in the soccer game. Each player is an energy source. As the players hit or kick the ball, they lose energy. The energy goes into the ball. The ball is the energy receiver. The ball moves because it receives energy from the players. The ball goes from source to receiver in order to do what the team wants it to do. They want to win the game by putting the ball into the other team's goal box.

The players are energy sources for the ball. The players receive their energy from the chemical energy of the food they eat. What is the energy source for the food?

The major source for all energy on Earth is the sun. Without solar energy, we would not have any plants to eat. We would not have any meat to eat without solar energy. Why not?

The Flow of Energy

Energy flows from a source to a receiver. The flow of energy from a source to a receiver is called **energy transfer.** Transfer means to move or flow from one object or person to another. You can easily observe the effects of energy transfer in the picture below.

Activity

How Is Energy Transferred?

What to use:

golf ball
grooved ruler
plastic margarine bowl

2 or 3 books
meter stick
pencil and paper

What to do:

1. Ask your teacher for a precut margarine bowl.

2. Place one book on the table. Use a ruler to make a ramp against the book.

3. Place the bowl upside down at the bottom of the ramp. Have the hole facing the ramp.

4. Hold the ball on the groove at the top of the ramp. Let the ball roll down the ramp. It should go through the hole into the bowl. Observe carefully. Measure and record how far the bowl slides.

5. Add a second book and repeat step 4. Add a third book and repeat step 4. Measure and record the results each time. Graph your results.

What did you learn?

1. What was the energy source?

2. What was the energy receiver?

3. How far did the bowl slide with one book? two? three?

Using what you learned:

1. How did you know that energy was transferred from a source to a receiver?

2. The ball at the top of the ramp has energy. Where does the ball get its energy?

3. When the bowl moves, it has energy. Where does it get its energy?

Energy flows from a source to a receiver in many ways. Sound energy is transferred by vibrating particles of matter. Sound energy can be transferred through solids, liquids, and gases. Light energy is transferred in waves. These waves of light energy can travel through some matter.

Electricity is a form of energy **that** must be transferred to be useful. Think about electric energy when you turn on an electric lamp. Charged particles flow from the outlet, through a wire, to the bulb. The charged particles are in motion. Electric energy is transferred by the motion of matter. Electric energy is transferred much like the energy was transferred in the soccer game.

Making Sure

1. What is energy transfer?
2. If you eat a sandwich, how is energy being transferred?

Heat Energy Transfer

Like other types of energy, heat flows from a source to a receiver. Think about bread baking in an oven. What is the energy receiver? What is the energy source? Heat energy always flows from matter of a higher temperature to matter of a lower temperature.

Heat energy can be transferred from a source to a receiver in three ways. One way is by conduction (kun DUK shun). **Conduction** takes place when heat is transferred by direct contact. A pan on the stove gets hot by conduction. The pan is touching or is in direct contact with the heat source. The pan is heated by conduction. How is the food in the pan heated? What is the heat source for the food? Why are potholders useful?

Heater

A second way that heat is transferred is by convection (kun VEK shun). **Convection** is the transfer of heat energy by the movement of heated gases or liquids. Look at the picture above. The air in the room is being heated by convection. You know that air is made of particles. Energy is transferred to the air above the furnace as it is heated.

249

The particles of heated air must have more energy than the unheated air in the room. The particles have more motion and move farther apart from each other. The movement causes the density of the warm air to become less than the density of the cool air. The less dense heated air begins to rise. Cooler air moves into the space that is left by the rising air. The cooler air is heated and then it rises. Uneven heating causes an upward and downward movement or current. These currents are called convection currents. The heated air rises and later sinks as it cools. When this cooler air returns to a furnace, it is heated again. The process of convection begins all over again.

Convection occurs when liquids and gases are not the same temperature throughout. Water in a pan on the stove is heated by convection. The water on the bottom of the pan gets warmed first. Why? The hot water rises. Cooler water moves down to the bottom of the pan. This movement happens over and over. It causes a convection current. You can see a convection current when oatmeal or noodles are added to boiling water. Name other examples of heat transfer by convection.

Finally, the third way heat energy is transferred is by radiation (rayd ee AY shun). **Radiation** is the transfer of energy by waves. Radiation transfers energy from an energy source to an energy receiver. The waves are changed to heat energy by the energy receiver.

Heat and light energy are transferred to Earth from the sun by radiation. The radiant energy from the sun travels through space in waves. These waves are absorbed by the Earth. What is the energy source? What is the energy receiver? The surface of the Earth is warmed by radiation. When you sit in the sun, you are being heated by radiation. Your body is the energy receiver of the radiant energy.

In the picture above, the people are being warmed by the fire. They are receivers of heat energy. Some of the energy from the fire travels outward in waves. It is transferred to the people by radiation. They do not have to put their hands close to or above the fire to feel the warmth. How would energy be transferred to your hand if you accidentally touched the fire? In what way is the heat transferred to the air directly above the fire?

Look at the pictures here. What are the energy sources and receivers? Find examples of heat transfer by conduction, convection, and radiation.

Activity

What Makes a Good Radiator?

What to use:

2 soup cans	thermometer	hot pad
water	measuring cup	pencil and paper

What to do:

Part A

1. Copy the chart below.

Water Temperatures of Cans (°C)				
		Black Can		Silver Can
Time in Minutes		Cool water	Hot water	Cool water	Hot water
	30				
	25				
	20				
	15				
	10				
	5				
	0				

2. Use one black and one silver can. Fill each ⅔ full of cool water. Measure the water temperature in each can to make sure they are the same.

3. Place each can in the bright sunlight. Predict which can of water will heat faster.

4. Observe and record the water temperature of each can every 5 minutes for 30 minutes.

Part B

1. Empty each soup can and use a hot pad to hold each can while you fill it with hot tap water.

2. Measure and record the water temperature of each can to make sure they are the same.

3. Place the cans on a table but <u>not</u> in the bright sunlight. Predict which can of water will cool faster.

4. Observe and record the water temperature of each can every 5 minutes for 30 minutes.

What did you learn?

1. In which soup can did the water heat faster?
2. In which soup can did the water cool faster?

Using what you learned:

1. What color, black or silver, seems to be the better radiator of heat energy?
2. What color clothing would be cooler to wear in warmer weather?

Energy Changes Form

Energy can move from place to place and change form. Radiant energy from the sun changes to heat energy when it is absorbed by matter. The body of a cat sitting in the sun absorbs radiant energy. How would the cat's body feel? Radiant energy from the sun is changed to heat energy.

Mechanical energy can also change to heat energy. An object in motion rubs against other objects causing friction. Friction makes heat.

You can feel heat from mechanical energy. Rub your hands together. You are producing heat energy. The harder and faster you rub your hands, the hotter they feel. Try rubbing an eraser quickly back and forth on a piece of paper. Gently touch the eraser. Feel the paper, too. How do they feel?

Look at the picture. What are they doing? Why might there be heat? Think of other times when mechanical energy changes to heat energy.

Energy Chains

Energy can change from one form to another form and then still to another. The transfer and change of energy from one form to another form is called an **energy chain.** As energy moves along the chain, each receiver becomes a source.

For example, think about a flashlight. You can trace the energy chains in a flashlight. When the flashlight is on, the chemicals in the batteries react. Chemical energy changes to electric energy in the batteries. The electric energy flows into the bulb. The bulb gives off light energy. You begin with chemical energy and end with light energy. Energy is transferred and changed in an energy chain. As energy moves along the chain, the energy receivers become energy sources.

Heat energy changes into mechanical energy in a gasoline engine. Heat causes the gases in a chamber to expand. When the gases expand, a piston is forced down and a crank turns. Heat can do work by changing into mechanical energy to move an object.

Eating food is part of an energy chain. Food has chemical energy. When you eat food, some of the chemical energy changes to heat energy. Your body needs heat energy to keep warm. When you walk or run, your body changes some chemical energy to

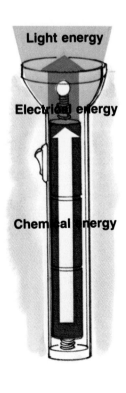

Light energy

Electric energy

Chemical energy

mechanical energy. The mechanical energy is the movement of your muscles.

Solar energy is radiant energy from the sun. Solar energy often is part of an energy chain. Solar energy can power satellites circling the Earth. Solar cells on a spacecraft change solar energy to electric energy. Electric energy changes to mechanical energy to power the spacecraft.

Energy chains are very useful to you. The pictures here show some energy chains. Trace the flow of energy in each energy chain. Which of these chains do you use? What energy chains can you find in your classroom and at school? See how many energy sources and receivers you can find.

People and Science

Taking Temperatures

When have you had your temperature taken? Perhaps you were ill with a cold or the flu. Your temperature helps your doctor know if there is a problem with your health. Human bodies have temperatures. Rocks and trees have temperatures, too. In fact, every object has a temperature because every object radiates heat energy. Heat energy cannot be seen, but it can be photographed with a special camera.

Mike Madison is a thermophotographer (thur moh foh TAHG ruh fur). Mike uses a special camera to take heat pictures, called thermograms (THUR muh gramz). Different temperatures appear as different colors in thermograms. Taking a thermogram of an object is like taking its temperature. Thermograms are used to spot many kinds of problems.

Mike uses thermograms to find energy leaks in buildings. As a thermophotographer, he can explain the meaning of the colors in thermograms. Lighter colors, such as yellow, show places where heat energy is escaping from buildings. Darker colors, such as red, show places where heat energy is staying inside. With this information Mike can tell people where they should insulate buildings to conserve heat energy. Mike likes his job because he helps people save money by conserving energy.

Chapter Review

Summary

- Energy transfer is the movement of energy from place-to-place.
- An energy source is a person or object that gives off energy.
- An energy receiver is a person or object that receives energy.
- Conduction is the transfer of heat by direct contact.
- Convection is the transfer of heat by movement of a heated gas or liquid.
- Radiation is the transfer of energy by waves.
- Energy chains are formed as energy is transferred and changed from one form to another form.

Science Words

energy source	**conduction**	**radiation**
energy receiver	**convection**	**energy chain**
energy transfer		

Questions

1. Explain two ways in which energy can be transferred.
2. When are you an energy source? When are you an energy receiver?
3. How is heat energy transferred by convection?
4. How is convection different from radiation?
5. What are energy chains? Give one example.
6. How is energy transferred when you play a piano?
7. Explain the energy chain involved when you eat some cheese.
8. What is conduction?
9. When you fry an egg, how is the heat energy transferred to the egg? How do you know?
10. How is solar energy a part of a food chain?

Chapter Three
Energy and Your Future

How do people use energy? Why should people save energy? How can you save energy?

Tina needed ten dollars to go on a weekend trip with her class. She was trying to earn and save money. Tina had already saved four dollars. By raking leaves, Tina earned three dollars more. Then she earned four dollars more by helping her sister on her paper route. Finally, Tina had eleven dollars.

Before the trip, Tina's friend called and asked her to go to the movie. Tina spent two dollars on the show and one dollar for snacks. Tina no longer had enough money for the class trip.

Conserving Energy

Tina should have been more careful about what she did and how much she spent. If she had conserved (kun SURVD) some of her money, she would have been able to go on the trip. **Conserving** means saving part of something and not wasting it. When you conserve, you have some left to use later.

Conserving energy is like conserving money. Once you use energy, it is gone. Then you have to obtain more. It is very important not to waste energy. You must use energy wisely in order to conserve it.

Energy from Fuel

People use large amounts of energy. We use energy to do work. We use energy to heat and cool homes and other buildings. People also use large amounts of energy for transportation. How do you and your family use energy?

Much of the energy we use is chemical energy. When fuel is burned, stored chemical energy is released as heat energy. Fuels are sources of energy that can be used only once. Most fuels are not easily or quickly replaced.

The fuels used most often today are coal, oil, and natural gas. These fuels take millions of years to form. People use more of these fuels every year and supplies are limited. No one knows for sure when we will run out of coal, oil, and natural gas. Some people think it may be soon. If we conserve the fuel we have now, there may be enough to last for a longer time.

Energy for Heating and Cooling

Much of the energy people use today is for heating and cooling buildings. Climate affects the amount of energy used for heating and cooling. In which climates might you use less energy to heat your home in winter? In which climates might you use more energy for cooling your home? During which seasons would you use more energy for cooling than heating?

Most of our energy for heating and cooling homes and buildings comes from burning fuels. The heat energy is released from fuels when they are burned. The heat is transferred to the air.

Natural gas and fuel oil are common fuels used for heating buildings. Often, heat energy from natural gas and fuel oil is changed to electric energy. Coal also is used to produce electric energy. Electric energy is used to heat or cool the air in buildings. Sometimes just the heat energy from coal is used to warm the air of large buildings and factories.

We can also use solar energy to heat buildings. In climates where the winters are not very cold, solar energy can be used to completely heat buildings. In very cold climates, solar energy can be used to supply some of the heat energy. Other fuels can be used along with solar energy to help warm buildings. Using solar energy with other fuels helps conserve the fuels.

What kinds of energy are used to heat and cool your home? Ask an adult to show you the heating or cooling system in your school. How does the system work? What kind of fuel does it use?

Controlling Temperature

One way to save energy is to control the temperature. Temperature can be controlled with thermostats (THUR muh stats). **Thermostats** are switches that control heating and cooling systems. You can set a thermostat at any comfortable temperature. Suppose you set a thermostat at 20°C. A thermostat measures the temperature in a room. When the room temperature goes below 20°C, the thermostat automatically turns on the heater. When the room temperature reaches 20°C, the thermostat turns off the heater. In this way, the thermostat controls the room temperature. Thermostats are also used to control cooling systems in buildings. Suppose the thermostat is set at 25°C. When the temperature in the room goes above 25°C, the thermostat turns on the cooling system. When the room temperature reads 25°C again, the thermostat turns off the cooling system. Find out where the thermostat is in your home. At what temperature is it set?

There may not always be enough fuel on Earth to provide energy for heating and cooling. Scientists are studying the fuel problem. They are looking for new sources of energy. Finding new sources of energy takes much time and money. What can you do now to conserve the energy sources we have?

One way to conserve some energy is to reduce the temperature of our buildings. We know it takes more heat energy to keep a building at 22°C than it does at 20°C. By reducing the temperature, less fuel is used. The person in the picture is lowering the thermostat from 22°C to 20°C. Some people set their thermostat at temperatures below 20°C at night when they are sleeping. Some thermostats will automatically lower the temperature during the night and raise it during the day. People can wear sweaters to keep warm during the day. There are many ways to be comfortable and conserve energy.

Another way people can conserve energy is to use proper insulation (ihn suh LAY shun) in their homes. **Insulation** is a substance that reduces the transfer of heat. In winter, insulation in the walls and ceiling of your home keeps the heat inside. Most people put more insulation in the ceiling of their home than in the walls. Why do you think insulation is more important in the ceiling than in the walls?

Insulation also keeps houses cooler in the summer. Less energy is needed to cool a house with enough insulation. Why do you think this is so? In the summer, what is the source of heat energy? What is the heat energy receiver?

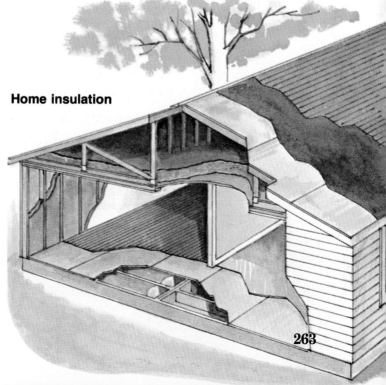

Home insulation

263

Activity

How Can You Insulate an Ice Cube?

What to use:

ice cube   other materials from your teacher
small dish   pencil and paper
insulation

What to do:

1. Make a plan for using the materials to insulate an ice cube.

2. Carry out your plan to insulate your ice cube. Use a small dish to catch the melted ice water.

3. Set the insulated ice cube aside. Observe the cube every 3 minutes for 30 minutes or until it melts.

What did you learn?

1. Which ice cube took the longest time to melt?

2. In your class, what kind of insulation protected the longest lasting ice cube?

3. What are some ways that can be used to make an ice cube melt quickly?

Using what you learned:

1. What are some materials that seem to make good insulators?

2. How could you keep a lunch of lemonade and potato salad cold?

When you wear a coat or a jacket in cold weather, you are using insulation. The jacket keeps the heat from quickly escaping your body. You are insulating your body. Why is it helpful to wear a hat or some covering on your head in cold weather?

Activity

How Can You Find Energy Leaks?

What to use:

pencil   tape

plastic food wrap   pencil and paper

Draft detector

What to do:

1. Make a "draft detector" by taping a sheet of plastic food wrap to a pencil as shown.

2. Test your draft detector by gently blowing on it. You should see the plastic flutter.

3. Test your classroom for energy leaks. Hold your draft detector where you think air might leak.

What did you learn?

1. Where did you discover energy leaks?

2. Which way was the air moving at each location?

Using what you learned:

1. Take your draft detector home and test for energy leaks.

2. Using your results, think of a plan to conserve energy in your home.

In some buildings, heat passes through small cracks around windows and doors. The small cracks cause air currents, or drafts. Drafts can be prevented by filling the cracks with putty. Putty, or caulking (KAWK ing), prevents heat from escaping through cracks. It costs very little money to put caulking around doors and windows.

Activity

How Would You Insulate a House?

What to use:

scissors   hot water
shoe box   hot pad
2 thermometers   margarine tub with lid
plastic food wrap   masking tape
newspapers   metric ruler
other insulating materials   pencil and paper

What to do:

1. Choose a team with which to work. Using a shoe box, have your team design and build a house that will not lose its heat rapidly. Your house must have 300 square cm of window space.

2. Cover each window with plastic wrap. Insulate your house with the material provided by your teacher.

3. Use a hot pad to fill your margarine tub with hot tap water, cover, and place the tub inside the house.

4. Place the thermometer inside the house so that it can be read through one of the windows. Seal the shoe box top on the house with masking tape.

5. On the chart, record the temperature of the air inside the house every 10 to 15 minutes for an hour.

6. Use the second thermometer to find the temperature outside the house every 10 to 15 minutes for an hour.

What did you learn?

1. What served as a furnace in the house?
2. What did you observe about the temperature inside the house?
3. After an hour, how did the temperature inside your house compare with the temperature of the room? How long would a box without any insulation stay warm? Try it.
4. How did the design of your house help conserve energy?

Using what you learned:

1. What changes, if any, would you make to keep your house cool when you put it on a sunny shelf?
2. For houses with the same number and size rooms, which would be easier to heat, a one-story or a two-story house? Why?

Many people are adding more insulation to their homes to help conserve energy. The more insulation a house has, the less heat will transfer in or out of it. How do you think adding insulation can save fuel, energy, and money?

Making Sure

1. Why is it necessary to conserve energy now?
2. How does insulation help conserve energy?

Energy for Transportation

About one-fourth of all energy used is for transportation. Cars, trucks, boats, planes, and trains are used to move people and materials.

In some cities, electric energy is used to run trains and buses. Yet, most energy for transportation comes from burning fuels. Most of these fuels are made from petroleum (puh TRO lee um). **Petroleum** is a thick liquid pumped out of the ground. Sometimes it is called crude oil. Gasoline for cars, trucks, and buses is made from petroleum. We are using petroleum very fast and soon we may run out of it. If we want to save some petroleum for later, we should conserve it now.

Many people are trying to conserve gasoline by riding bikes or walking. Instead of driving alone to work or school, people form car pools. Several people can ride together and take turns driving in car pools. People can conserve energy by riding trains and buses, too. For instance, thirty people would use far less energy if they all rode in one bus instead of driving thirty cars!

The cost of gasoline is increasing. Many people buy cars that are smaller, lighter, and use less fuel. It takes less energy to move a light object than it does a heavy one. Why? Car makers are designing smaller cars that will go farther using less gas. How will smaller cars help conserve gas?

Daily Energy Use

We know that people today use most energy for heating, cooling, and transporting. Many people are trying to conserve energy.

Everyone can conserve energy. You are the most important person in conserving energy. Here are some ways to conserve energy. What others can you add to the list?

1. Conserve heat.

   Keep outside doors and windows closed tightly. Ask your parents about the setting on your thermostat. Wear warm clothes for comfort at lower temperatures.

2. Conserve water.

   Do not let water run all the time while you wash your hands or brush your teeth. Turn the water off when you do not need it. Use hot water only when you really need it. Take short showers instead of baths.

3. Conserve electricity.

   Use appliances that are not electric when possible. Each time you open the refrigerator, large amounts of energy are used. Before you open the refrigerator door, decide what you want to take out. Then you will not need to have the door open for long. Use sunlight for lighting when possible. Turn off lights when they are not needed. Try to find entertainment without using electricity. For instance, suggest your family play a game together instead of watching television.

4. Conserve gasoline.

   Ask your parents to drive you to places only when it is necessary. Some of your friends may be going to the same places. Ask if they would form a car pool with you. Walk or ride a bicycle to nearby places.

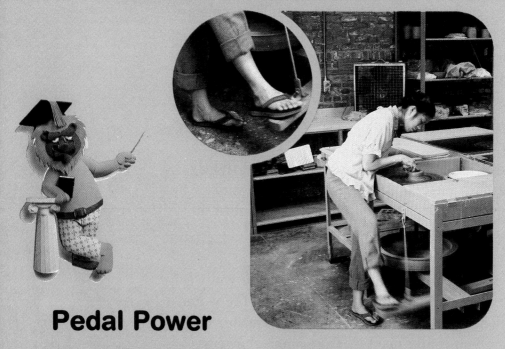

Pedal Power

If you enjoy riding a bicycle, you are not alone. Millions of people ride bikes for fun and exercise. Some people ride bikes to conserve energy, too. When you pedal a bike, you supply pedal power to make the bike move. Pedal power is a form of mechanical energy.

Bikes are a great way to get from place to place. What good is a bike that will not go anywhere? Pedal power can supply energy for many tasks besides moving from place to place. Pedaling bikes that will not move can supply energy to operate tools, pump water, and grind grain.

A long time ago many machines were operated with pedal power.

One example you may have seen is a treadle (TRED uhl) sewing machine. Sewing machines and most other machines today are operated by electric energy. However, some machines, such as a potter's wheel, are still operated with pedal power.

One man has thought of a way to use pedal power in his home. He was worried about his children's health. He thought they watched too much television and were not getting enough exercise. The man changed their television so that it can only be operated with pedal power. Now, the family must pedal a bicycle to supply energy for their television. In this way, they exercise and conserve energy, too!

■■■■■Chapter Review■

Summary

- If you conserve fuel now, there will be some left for the future.
- Coal, oil, and natural gas are the most widely used fuels, but they are not easily replaced.
- Most of the energy people use in their homes is for heating and cooling.
- Controlling temperature and adding insulation help to conserve energy in buildings.
- Gasoline is made from petroleum.
- Using appliances wisely helps conserve energy.
- Everyone can conserve energy.

Science Words

conserving	**insulation**
thermostats	**petroleum**

Questions

1. How is conserving energy like conserving food?
2. For what do people use fuels most often?
3. Explain how people can conserve energy used for heating or cooling.
4. How do car pools conserve energy?
5. Name one way you can conserve energy at home and at school.
6. How can a thermostat help conserve energy for heating and cooling?
7. Why should you consider how high on a wall you place a thermostat?
8. Make two lists. Include all of the home appliances you need on one list. Include appliances that you do not need on the other list. Tell why you put each appliance on each list.

✓ Self Checks

Answer these Self Checks on a sheet of paper.

1. List five ways people waste energy.
2. List two types of energy and explain how each differs.
3. Heat energy is transferred in what three ways?
4. Explain the energy chain in eating lettuce.
5. Give one example of an energy chain in your life.
6. Name two examples of mechanical energy.
7. Name the energy source and receiver in each picture below.
8. Each picture below shows energy changing forms. What forms are involved in each?

a

b

▢ Idea Corner
More Fun with Science

1. Keep a daily journal of the ways you use energy. Count the energy transfers and changes involved. Report the results to your class.

2. Build a mobile using pictures that show the different forms of energy.

3. Write a story about all the ways you have used energy today. Underline the verbs that show energy was used. Above each verb write the energy forms used. Example:

   electric

   I <u>toasted</u> bread for breakfast.

4. Devise an energy plan for your home. Explain the plan to your family. Ask for suggestions to help conserve energy. Put your plan into use.

Reading for Fun

The Alaska Pipeline by Virginia O. Shumaker, Julian Messner: New York, © 1979.

   The Alaska pipeline story tells how the oil from Alaska is routed to us.

Coal in the Energy Crisis by Charles Coombs, William Morrow & Co.: New York, © 1980.

   Find out about the coal use of today and how it will change for tomorrow.

Sunpower by Norman F. Smith, Coward, McCann and Geoghegan, Inc.: New York, © 1976.

   Find out how all our energy comes directly or indirectly from the sun.

Unit 8

Exploring Earth Patterns

Chapter One
The Earth's Layers

What is under the Earth's surface? Why do scientists study earthquakes and volcanoes? How do scientists learn about the inside of the Earth?

How can you guess what your birthday gift is before you open the package? What might you do to get the information? You can study the size and shape of the package. You might guess its mass by lifting it. How can you tell whether the gift is hard or soft, small or large? All of these properties are clues to help you identify the gift inside the package.

Studying the Earth

Scientists have the same type of problem when they study the Earth. The inside of the Earth is like the birthday gift. The surface of the Earth is like the wrapping on the gift. Scientists can use direct observation to study the surface of the Earth. They can even measure its mass. They study changes on the Earth's surface for clues to what is inside the Earth. What kind of observation do they use to study the inside of the Earth?

After you finish your guessing game, you can open the birthday gift. Then you can see and feel what is inside. You know if your guess is right or wrong. Scientists have not been able to look deep inside the Earth.

Activity

How Do Scientists Find Out What Is Under the Earth's Crust?

What to use:

Earth's model box   metric ruler
drinking straw   pencil and paper

What to do:

1. Make a chart and a graph like the ones shown for each row of holes.

Hole Depth Chart					
Hole	A	B	C	D	E
Depth (cm)					

Hole Depth Graph					
Hole	A	B	C	D	E
Depth (cm) 0					
2					
4					
6					
8					
10					
12					

2. Use the first row of holes on the model box going from end to end across the box lid. Carefully probe the straw straight down into each hole until it stops.

3. Measure and record on the chart how deep the straw is able to go in each hole.

278

4. Record each hole's depth on the graph. Use your ruler to connect the points with a straight line.

5. Repeat steps 2 through 4 for each row of holes.

What did you learn?

1. How was the straw probe used to observe the inside of the box?

2. Describe the shape of the bottom of the box.

3. What could you do to gain more accurate information?

Using what you learned:

1. What senses did you use to observe the floor of the model box? Was this direct or indirect observation?

2. How is the inside of the Earth like the floor of the model box?

Scientists already have gathered much information about the inside of the Earth. They believe the Earth has three layers. They have given each layer a name. The outer or top layer of the Earth is the **crust.** The crust is very thin like the skin on an apple. Under the crust is a thicker layer called the **mantle.** The area in the center of the Earth is called the **core.** The core is very hot. The density of the core is greater than the density of the crust and mantle.

Crust

The surface of the Earth where you live is the top part of the crust. The crust is the only layer of the Earth you can see. The crust is like a thin shell covering the Earth. It is from 8 to 64 km thick. The distance of 64 km is about the distance you would travel in 45 minutes when driving at 85 km per hour.

Igneous, sedimentary, and metamorphic rocks make up the crust. Igneous rocks form from hot, liquid rock, or magma. Where on the Earth does magma cool to form igneous rocks? Sedimentary rocks form when layers of Earth materials are deposited and hardened from the pressure of material on top of them. Metamorphic rocks were once igneous or sedimentary rocks. Heat and pressure in the Earth's crust changed them into metamorphic rocks.

Mantle and Core

It is hard to imagine what something you have never seen looks like. Many years ago, some people believed the Earth was hollow. Others believed you could tunnel straight through the Earth from one side to the other. Coal mines dug by people and machines are very shallow compared to the thickness of the crust. Even the deepest oil wells do not go all the way through the crust.

Today geologists know more about the inside of the Earth. They think the mantle is mostly solid rock and is about 2900 km thick. A distance of 2900 km is about the distance between New York and

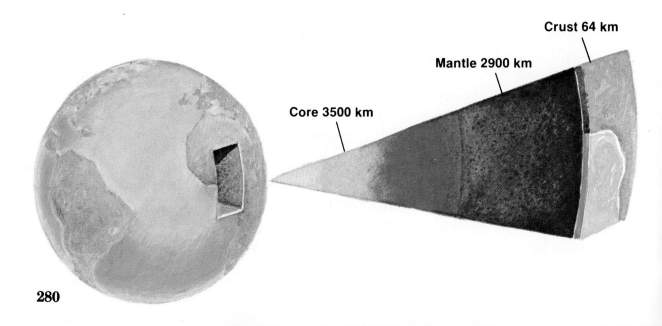

Core 3500 km

Mantle 2900 km

Crust 64 km

Colorado. The density of mantle rock is greater than the density of rocks in the crust. Geologists also believe the mantle is very hot. The temperature may range from 900°C to 2000°C.

Geologists think the core of the Earth is shaped like a ball. It may be about 7000 km thick. Some of the core may be made of metal elements such as iron and nickel. Part of the core may be like a liquid. The core is hotter than the mantle. Scientists believe the temperature is about 5000°C in some places.

Geologists would like to learn more about the mantle and the core. Since it is not possible to travel deep into the Earth to observe, geologists must make indirect observations. There are many clues that geologists can study to make indirect observations.

Making Sure

1. Name the three layers of the Earth.
2. What happens to the temperature of the Earth between its crust and its center?

Clues from Volcanoes

Volcanoes provide important clues about the crust. **Volcanoes** are openings in the Earth's crust through which magma flows. Heat and pressure in certain areas of the crust build up to force out magma. Sometimes the pressure forces magma out of the Earth rapidly. At other times magma is squeezed from the crust like toothpaste from a tube.

Magma that flows from volcanoes is called lava. Geologists learn about the temperature inside the crust by studying lava. How do you think geologists know about the temperature of the mantle and core?

Geologists observed that volcanoes seem to occur near earthquakes. Study the map below of the world's volcanoes and earthquake zones. Why do you think most volcanoes and earthquakes occur near each other?

Clues from Earthquakes

Earthquakes provide more clues to the inside of the Earth. **Earthquakes** are movements of large areas of rock. Changes in the Earth's crust can cause earthquakes.

Rocks deep in the Earth's crust are under much pressure. Some of the pressure is caused by the rocks above. Slow, steady pressure causes rock layers to bend. Other sudden pressure may cause rock layers to break or crack.

Sometimes the broken parts move past each other along the break. They may slide past each other sideways or up and down. The break along which the broken rock layers move is called a **fault.** An

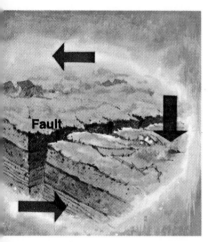

Fault

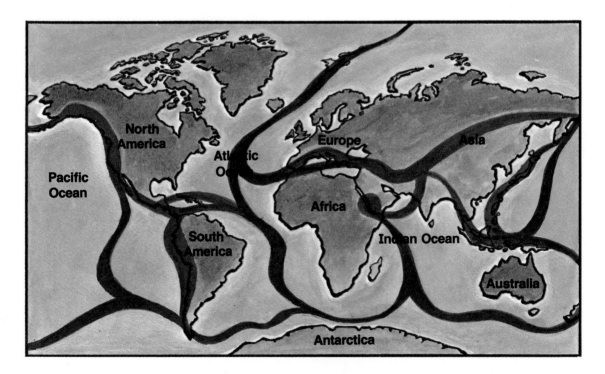

earthquake occurs along a fault. The famous San Andreas Fault is in California. Movement along the San Andreas Fault has caused many earthquakes. The picture on this page shows the San Andreas Fault. How can you tell movement has taken place?

San Andreas Fault, California

When the Earth trembles and shakes in an earthquake, shock waves are produced. You can sense a kind of shock wave when you hit a table with your hand. You can feel the wave on any part of the table.

An earthquake causes three different kinds of shock waves. The shock waves travel out in all directions from the earthquake center. Each type of wave travels through rock at a different speed and in a different way. Earthquake waves speed up, slow down, and bend as they travel through different rocks. Scientists measure the force of the shock waves with instruments called **seismographs** (SIZE muh grafs). The records from seismographs lead scientists to believe the mantle and core of the Earth are made of different materials.

There are many seismographs throughout the world. Each measures and records movements of the Earth's rock layers. Scientists study the information to find where earthquakes are occurring. They use seismographs to measure the energy of earthquakes.

Scientists compare the energy of earthquakes with the Richter scale. The **Richter** (RIHK tur) **scale** is a series of numbers from zero to nine. Shock waves from each earthquake are compared using the Richter scale.

Earthquake Effects and the Richter Scale	
Richter Scale Reading	Comments
0 to 2.5	Generally not felt but recorded
3.0 to 4.5	Local damage
5.0 to 6.5	Can be destructive in heavily populated area
7.0 to 8.0	Major earthquakes Cause serious damage About 10 occur each year
8.0 and over	Great earthquakes Occur once every 5 to 10 years Cause total destruction to communities

Earthquake Effects

People hardly notice some earthquakes. Minor earthquakes are rated less than seven on the Richter scale. Earthquakes with ratings seven or above are called major earthquakes. Major earthquakes cause much damage as the ground trembles and shakes. Buildings tumble to the ground. Large rocks are jarred loose and slide down mountains. Trees may fall. People may be badly hurt from falling buildings, rocks, or trees.

Besides falling objects, fire is a great danger in an earthquake. Fire occurs, gas pipes break, and electric lines fall. Sometimes earthquakes cause huge sea waves. The huge waves crash onto the land, destroying objects with their force and water.

Geologists are trying to learn more about earthquakes. They want to be able to warn people when an earthquake is going to occur. Often, they study the history of other earthquakes to guess when an area may have an earthquake.

There are several signs geologists look for in predicting an earthquake. Some rocks deep in the ground may begin to tremble before an earthquake occurs. Gases also may escape from below the ground. Most people are not able to feel the slight rock movement or smell the gases. Some animals, such as cats and dogs, can feel the trembling of the Earth. It is believed that horses can sense the gases. The animals may begin to act differently. Geologists observe the unusual behavior of other animals, too. They also use instruments to detect the rock movement and gases.

Blowing Its Top

Imagine a blast 500 times greater than an atomic bomb blast. In 1980, a volcano in the state of Washington made such a blast. The volcano, Mount St. Helens, blew up and provided a spectacular sight. Sadly, the eruption caused much damage over thousands of kilometers.

What is it like to be near a volcano when it blows its top? Hundreds of people know. They felt, saw, and heard several eruptions.

Seconds after the eruption, gas, fire, ash, and rock filled the air. Less than an hour later dark, ash-filled clouds rose into the once peaceful, clear air. Days later, hundreds of kilometers away, people dusted, pushed, and shoveled ash from their windows, cars, and streets.

Lives of some people were lost in the eruption. Daring rescue efforts were made to save many lives. Now many people fear living in the area of Mount St. Helens. Others are trying to rebuild their homes and businesses hoping the volcano will not cause more damage.

Scientists cannot be sure how long the volcano will continue to erupt. No one has an answer. Some scientists expect the volcano to continue erupting for 25 years. What do you think?

Chapter Review

Summary

- Geologists use direct and indirect observations to study the Earth.
- The surface of the Earth is part of the crust.
- The mantle is an Earth layer of mostly solid rock.
- The core is the center of the Earth.
- Scientists study volcanoes and earthquakes to learn about the inside of the Earth.
- A break or crack in the Earth's crust is called a fault.
- Seismographs are instruments geologists use to measure the amount of energy of earthquakes.
- The earthquake's energy is compared using a Richter scale.

Science Words

crust	**core**	**earthquakes**	**seismographs**
mantle	**volcanoes**	**fault**	**Richter scale**

Questions

1. Describe the Earth's crust.
2. How are the crust and mantle different?
3. Which is the hottest layer of the Earth?
4. What clues about the Earth's crust do volcanoes provide scientists?
5. What causes earthquakes?
6. How are igneous, sedimentary, and metamorphic rocks different from each other?
7. How are volcanoes formed?
8. How is knowing about faults important to the study of earthquakes?
9. What kind of earthquake would have a Richter scale rating of over 8?
10. In what way are seismographs helpful to geologists?

Chapter Two

The Changing Surface

How does the Earth's surface change? How quickly do the changes happen? What patterns are caused by the changes?

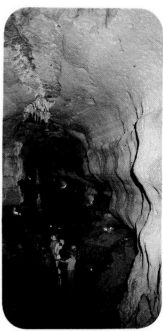

Pictures can show us how the surface of the Earth looks. What does each picture show?

Landscape and Time

A **landscape** is a part of the surface of the Earth that you can see. The landscape may have plants, rocks, mountains, and valleys. Observe the Earth landscapes shown here. How do these landscapes differ from the landscape near your home? Where might you go to find a landscape like each of these? Which one is the most different?

A landscape is always changing. Suppose you make a picture of a certain landscape today. In five years you can return to the same place to make another picture. You might find the landscape has changed. Suppose you make pictures of the same landscape each day until you are in high school. You might not notice the landscape is changing day to day. Sometimes landscape changes occur so slowly that you may not notice them.

At other times a landscape changes very fast. Suddenly we notice the landscape looks different. What landscapes do you know that change quickly? How do people change landscapes? When are these changes fast? When are these changes slow?

The Agents of Change

Landscapes are changed by weathering and erosion (ih ROH zhun). **Weathering** is the breaking of rocks into smaller pieces. **Erosion** is the carrying away of rocks and soil. Weathering and erosion act together to change the landscape.

Flowing stream

Ocean waves

Groundwater

Glacier

Sand dunes

The causes of erosion are called **agents of change.** Running water, groundwater, wave action of water, glaciers, and wind cause erosion. They are agents of change. Agents of change can move material from place to place. They also can drop or deposit material. **Deposition** (dep uh ZIHSH un) is the dropping or laying down of rocks and soil. What is the agent of change in each picture?

Activity

How Does Running Water Change a Landscape?

What to use:

sand
sprinkling can
large flat pan
water

2 or 3 blocks of wood
marking pens
pencil and paper

What to do:

1. Make a landscape with a hill of damp sand on one end of the pan. Leave at least half the pan empty to collect water. Draw a picture of the landscape.

2. Place the blocks under the hill end of the pan.

3. Use the sprinkling can with water to make a slow, steady rain on the hill.

4. Record the changes you observe. Draw a picture of the new landscape.

What did you learn?

1. Where did erosion occur in your landscape?
2. Where did deposition take place?
3. What does erosion do to the landscape?
4. What does deposition do to the landscape?

Using what you learned:

1. Describe how you think a landscape would look after many years of erosion.
2. What would happen to the amount of erosion and deposition if a landscape were more sloped?
3. What would happen to the amount of erosion and deposition if a landscape were nearly flat? Plan, experiment, and test your predictions.

Running Water

Running water is the most common agent of change. It changes a landscape by both erosion and deposition. Some of the water from rain and melting snow soaks into the soil. The rest of the water flows over the surface and moves downhill. What causes the water to move downhill? Running water moves soil and rocks to rivers and streams.

Running water carries rocks and soil in different ways. Small amounts of rock and soil dissolve in the water. Some substances do not dissolve in water. They cause the water to look cloudy. Other substances are pushed, rolled, or bounced along the bottom of the stream. What size particles do you think are easiest for a river to move?

Running water changes the landscape by depositing Earth materials. The deposited materials are called **sediments.** Deposition occurs when running water slows down or evaporates. Slow running water has less energy than fast running water. It can no longer carry as much sediment. The water deposits or drops the sediments.

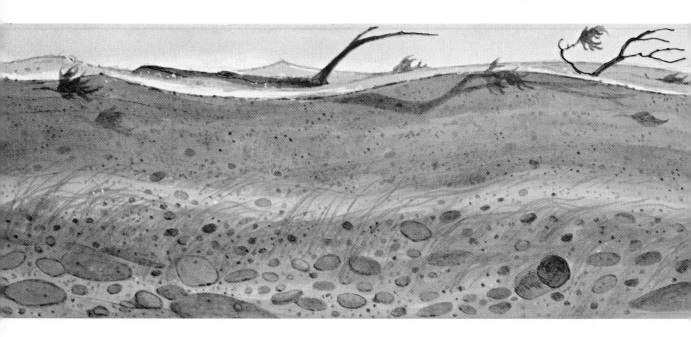

The sediments are deposited in a certain order. Large sediments are pushed, rolled, or bounced along the stream bottom and are deposited first. Smaller sediments that are not dissolved in the water are deposited second. The water must be calm before these sediments are deposited. They take more time to settle to the bottom. Why do you think this is true? The third and last sediments to be deposited are those that are dissolved. They are deposited when the water evaporates.

Layers of sediments are deposited in streams, rivers, lakes, and along seacoasts. Later these Earth materials may be buried by other sediments. After many years they may become sedimentary rocks.

Making Sure

1. How are weathering and erosion different?
2. How do agents of change work to change the landscape?
3. What agents of change move rocks and soil?

Activity

How Are Sediments Deposited in Calm Water?

What to use:

large baby food jar with lid   large spoon
sand   hand lens
soil   colored pencils
water   pencil and paper

What to do:

1. Put 2 spoonfuls of soil and 1 spoonful of sand into the jar.

2. Fill the jar about 2/3 full of water. Twist the jar lid on firmly.

3. Shake the jar well.

4. Place the jar on your desk and use the hand lens to observe the closed jar carefully for several minutes.

5. Use your colored pencils to draw a picture of the jar of water and sediments.

What did you learn?

1. Describe how the water, soil, and sand mixture looked when you first put the jar down.

2. How did the mixture change as you observed it?

3. Which particles settled first, soil or sand?

Using what you learned:

1. How does the size of the sediments that settled first compare with the size of the sediments that settled later?

2. Where could you see sediments like these deposited in nature?

Groundwater

Both rain and melted snow can soak into the ground. The water moves into tiny spaces between soil particles. Water also soaks into some kinds of rock. Water trapped in soil and rock spaces is called **groundwater.** Groundwater is an agent of change.

Some rocks are eroded by groundwater. Certain minerals that make up rocks dissolve in groundwater. Then the rocks become weak and crumbly. In time, the rocks break apart. Holes, pits, and caves can be formed by groundwater.

Groundwater can change a landscape in another way. When groundwater evaporates, the dissolved minerals are left behind. Mineral deposits are sometimes found in caves or in rock cracks. Minerals can also be deposited in low places in fields.

Floods and Waves

Sometimes water cannot soak into the ground fast enough. It runs off the soil into streams and rivers.

The streams and rivers become full and overflow or flood. A flood is an agent of change. Floods erode a landscape. Many sediments are moved in floods. Floods deposit these sediments where the water slows down. Is a flood a fast or slow agent of change for a landscape?

Water changes a landscape with waves, too. Wave action is an agent of change. Wave action causes erosion. Waves crash into rocks and break them apart. It may take a long time for rocks to break into smaller pieces. The broken rocks may be carried back and forth by the waves until they become sand. The sand also is moved around by waves. Moving sand helps to wear down other rocks.

Ice Changes a Landscape

Glaciers (GLAY shurz) change a landscape. Glaciers are large masses of ice that move very slowly. The movement of glaciers causes erosion.

Because of their size and mass, glaciers crush the rocks under them as they move over a landscape. Some of the broken rocks are pushed or carried with the glaciers. Some rocks and soil are frozen in the glacier ice. Others are carried on top of the ice. The rocks and soil are deposited when the glaciers stop moving. When glaciers melt, rocks and soil are carried and then deposited by running water from the glaciers. Glaciers change a landscape by both erosion and deposition. It takes many years before landscape changes from glaciers are seen.

Dust storm

Wind Changes the Landscape

Wind erosion happens most in areas with few trees or plants. These areas are usually dry. The rocks and soil are loose. Where could you see areas like this? Small rocks and soil are carried away by the wind. Strong wind blowing across the surface picks up pieces of dust and sand. They may be blown very high. They may be carried for long distances. This leaves the landscape changed. Think of some landscapes that have been eroded by wind.

In a dust storm the wind carries dust high into the air. When the wind stops blowing, the dust slowly falls to the ground. This settling of dust is an example of depositing. It may take several days. The change seems slow. How is settling dust like sediments deposited by running water?

Chapter Review

Summary

- A landscape is part of the Earth's surface.
- Landscape changes may be fast or slow.
- Weathering, erosion, and deposition cause landscape changes.
- Water, wind, and ice are agents of change of a landscape.
- Erosion occurs when rocks and soil are carried away.
- Deposition occurs when rocks and soil are laid down.
- Running water changes the landscape by erosion and deposition.
- Groundwater can dissolve minerals in rocks and deposit them in another place.
- Floods move sediments to change the landscape quickly.
- Waves cause the erosion of rocks and sand.
- Wind erosion occurs in dry areas where few plants grow.

Science Words

landscape	agents of change	sediments
weathering	deposition	groundwater
erosion		

Questions

1. Name one landscape change that occurs rapidly.
2. Name two landscape changes that occur slowly.
3. List the agents of change. How does each one change a landscape?
4. In what order are sediments deposited by a stream flowing into a lake?
5. What landscape changes have taken place near your school?
6. How is weathering different from erosion?
7. Explain how beaches are formed.
8. What agent of change is likely to cause erosion in a desert?

Chapter Three

Features of the Landscape

What do you see in this landscape? How are landscapes formed? Where might you go to see a landscape like this?

If you like swimming at a beach or hiking in the mountains, then landforms are important to you. Landforms can make landscapes very interesting. What landforms are near where you live? Many people travel to certain places to enjoy the landforms there. Maybe you will learn about some landforms that you would like to visit.

Landscape Features

Landforms are the features of a landscape. They appear as high places, low places, and curved places in the Earth's crust. Beaches and mountains are two kinds of landforms. What are some other landforms?

There are many different landforms. Scientists group landforms by the way they look and how they form. Agents of change such as water, wind, and ice help shape landforms. Other forces can produce landforms, too.

Mountains

Some landforms are formed when the crust is built up or raised higher. Others are formed when areas are made lower. Sometimes pressure pushes up areas to form mountains. **Mountains** are sections of the Earth's crust that are higher than nearby areas.

Mt. Rainier

Ship Rock

Geologists group mountain landforms by the way they are made. Some mountains are made by volcanoes. Volcanoes force ash and hot lava onto the Earth's surface. Then the lava and ash cool and become igneous rock. Over a long period of time, mountains can form in this way. What famous volcanic mountains do you know?

Sometimes strange landscapes form when the softer volcanic rock erodes faster than the harder volcanic rock. The harder rock is left standing high above the ground. Geologists believe Shiprock in New Mexico was formed this way.

Activity

How Can Faults Form Mountains?

What to use:

4 clay pieces
(use 4 different colors)
table knife

wood block
pencil and paper

What to do:

1. Make 4 different colored clay layers. Each should measure approximately 15 cm long by 5 cm wide by 2 cm high.

2. Place the layers on top of each other. Draw a picture of the layers.

3. Using the table knife, cut down through the layers at the angle shown forming 2 layered blocks.

4. Press the 2 blocks back together again so they stay together.

5. Place both clay blocks on the table edge so that one-half of it rests on the table. Hold the other half up with the wood block under it.

6. Hold both halves in place. Push down on the over-hanging block until some layers in the 2 clay stacks slide past each other.

7. Have your partner hold the stacks in place and observe them carefully. Draw a picture showing the layers after the stacks have moved.

What did you learn?

1. Which block moved down?

2. Compared to the lower block, which way did the other appear to move?

3. Where is the fault in your model?

Using what you learned:

1. In your model, you made a fault with the table knife. How is a fault made in the Earth's crust?

2. Which side would be like a mountain?

3. How can you use your model to show an earthquake?

4. How can faults make a mountain?

Other mountains formed when large blocks of crust, or fault blocks, moved along faults. Over a long period of time, hundreds of earthquakes lifted fault blocks high in the air. The Grand Tetons in Wyoming as well as the Sierra Nevadas (see ER uh · nuh VAD uz) in California are fault block mountains.

Sometimes pressure inside the Earth causes the crust to bend or fold. These folds were lifted to form mountains like the Appalachian (ap uh LAY chun) Mountains.

The Rocky Mountains were formed in all three ways. The Rocky Mountains are not simple. They have volcanoes, fault blocks, and folded layers. What mountains are nearest your home? How were they formed? What mountains would you like to visit?

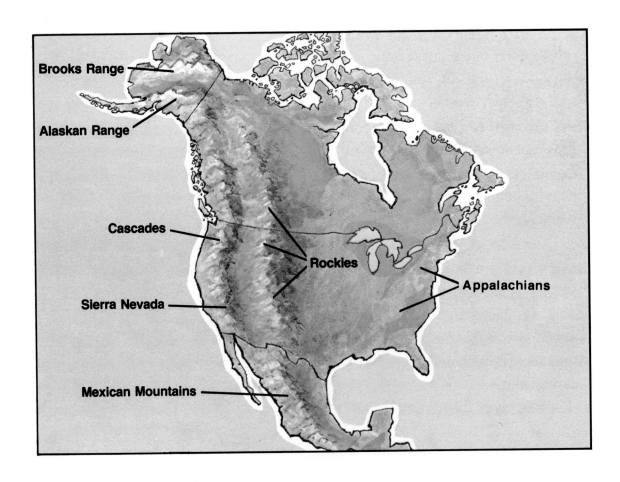

Coral reef

Coral

Coral Reefs

Some landforms are made by living things. The hollow-bodied animals, corals, can become landforms. Corals live in groups in clear, shallow, warm ocean water. The hard coverings of many corals become joined together. The coverings stay together even when the animals inside die. The group gets larger and larger. It becomes a landform called a coral reef. A **coral reef** is a landform made by thousands of coral coverings.

Some coral reefs are found near the shoreline of tropical islands. In the ocean, the reef grows from the bottom of the ocean up to the ocean's surface. Coral reefs may stick out of the water when the tide is low. They are often underwater at high tide.

Making Sure

1. What are landforms?
2. List three different ways mountains are formed.
3. What landform can be made by an animal?

Deposited minerals

Caves

Groundwater forms some interesting landforms under the ground. When some rocks beneath the soil dissolve in water, large empty spaces or **caves** form. Later, dripping water may evaporate and deposit minerals. The deposited minerals form unusual shapes on cave ceilings and floors. If you travel to New Mexico, you will be able to see the Carlsbad Caverns. They are very large. The unusual shapes were formed by groundwater. For thousands of years the groundwater dripped to form the shapes.

River Valleys and Plains

Some valleys are landforms caused by erosion. **Valleys** are low areas usually found between mountains. They are formed as rivers flow across and down the land. The running water erodes away rock and soil. It can form deep valleys with steep sides called **canyons.** Canyons form where rivers flow very fast. Some canyons are formed by streams that flow from mountains. Why do mountain streams form steep canyons?

Canyon

Imagine you are with your family in a very
famous canyon called the Grand Canyon. Each of
you is on a donkey, riding through land that was
eroded by the Colorado River. You notice the steep,
rocky, colorful sides of the canyon. You look far
below to see the river flowing quickly. Many people
come from far away just to look at this landform. If
you could come back in 100 years, how might the
river have changed the landscape?

Running water forms other landforms, too. Water
overflows river banks during floods. Then the river
covers all of the valley bottom. Floods change the
valley bottom by eroding and depositing soil.
Sediments deposited by floods make the valley
bottom flatter. This flat valley bottom along the
river is called a **floodplain.**

Floodplain

307

Floodplains are good places to grow crops. They have thick layers of rich soil. More soil material is deposited each time the river floods. In what other ways might floodplains be used? Why should people avoid building on floodplains?

When running water slows down, sediments in the water settle to the bottom of the river. Rivers slow down suddenly when they flow into lakes or oceans. The deposited sediments form a fan-shaped landform called a **delta.** The Mississippi River has a large delta at its end. Into what large body of water does the Mississippi River flow? What other large rivers have deltas?

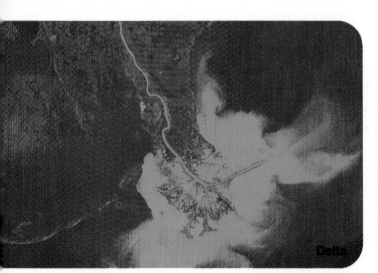

Delta

Badlands

Running water changes a landscape in dry places, too. Some rivers and streams contain water only when it rains. Rainwater runs off hills and slopes during heavy rains. It collects in small ditches and gulleys. Rainwater erodes loose rock and soil. Some landscapes have soft rock and few plants. Running water erodes these places into unusual shapes called **badlands.** The most famous badlands are in South Dakota. Why do you think these landforms are called badlands? What other agent of change might cause erosion in badlands?

Sand Dunes and Sandbars

Wind can form interesting landforms. Both erosion and deposition by wind produce changes in a landscape. Wind erodes by pushing or carrying sand and dust. Wind deposits the sand and dust to form a new landform.

When a lot of sand is deposited in the same place, a sand dune forms. **Sand dunes** are large hills of windblown sand. The wind also can carry away the sand of a dune. A dune may form in another place. The landscape changes again. Where would you expect to see sand dunes?

Wind erosion

Sand dunes

Sandbar in stream

Moving water forms sandbars in the same way wind forms sand dunes. **Sandbars** are piles of sand and rock deposited by moving water. Sandbars are often seen above the water's surface. They can be found in streams, rivers, and oceans. After a time, sandbars may form islands. Where in a stream would you find a sandbar? Why?

Sand is often washed up and deposited along the ocean shores. Large sandbars such as Miami Beach, Florida, are used and enjoyed by many people. Waves, tides, and winds can sometimes form sandbars into different shapes. The water and wind cause erosion and deposition. The coast of Massachusetts has several different types of sandbars.

 # Activity

How Do Waves Both Erode and Deposit Sand?

What to use:

long shallow cake pan
sand
pebbles
wood block

water
chalkboard
eraser or book
pencil and paper

What to do:

1. Make a model beach by putting a single layer of pebbles at one end of the pan. Cover the pebbles with a thick layer of sand.

2. Place the eraser or book under the beach end of the pan so that the pan slopes.

3. Slowly add water to the low end of the pan until it comes to the edge of the model beach.

4. Place the wood block in the pan in the low end. Move the block back and forth gently, making slow gentle waves.

5. Observe the beach area and record any changes.

6. Repeat steps 4 and 5. This time move the block faster making larger and stronger waves.

7. Observe the beach area and record any changes.

What did you learn?

1. How do gentle waves change the beach area?

2. How do strong waves change the beach area?

3. Observe and describe the motion of one or two sand grains. In what way is the sand moving?

Using what you learned:

1. Which step best represents the beach after a hurricane? Why do you think so?

2. How would strong winds from the ocean change the beach?

3. During which season of the year would you expect more erosion of the beach to occur? Why?

4. What effect would the steepness of the beach have on how quickly the sand moves?

Beaches

Waves can produce other landforms. Waves both erode and deposit sand. Imagine you are walking close to the water's edge. You hear and see the water gently hitting the shore. More than water is moving with the waves. Erosion and deposition are occurring while you are walking the beach. Both changes also occurred before you walked on the beach. Deposited sand or eroded rock formed the **beach.**

Sometimes storm waves carry away the beach sand. Then there is only rock along the shore. The beach is gone. Later, more gentle waves may deposit sand and form a new beach. At other times, waves weather the rock into fine sand to form a beach.

Landforms from Glaciers

Glaciers change the Earth's surface and form interesting landforms. Glaciers weather and erode rocks and soil from the sides of mountains and valleys. Valleys become smooth and rounded into U-shapes. How are glacier valleys different from river valleys?

Glaciers also form moraines (muh RAYNZ). **Moraines** are ridges of long, low piles of rock and soil. As glaciers melt they deposit the rocks, soil, and other materials they carried. Some moraines form in front of melting glaciers. They may block a valley like a dam. Water from the melting glacier becomes trapped behind the moraines to form a lake.

If you were a geologist you would look for scratches, grooves, and broken and deposited rocks as clues of glacier landforms. Even if you are not a geologist, you may find clues that glaciers once passed over some land. U-shaped valleys and moraines are landforms caused by glaciers.

Glacial scratches

Moraine

People and Science

Underground Exploring

Why would you want to crawl into a hole in a hillside? For a long time some people have explored caves. These people are called spelunkers. Spelunca is the Latin word for cave.

One of the most famous spelunkers was Jim White of Carlsbad, New Mexico. In 1901, when Jim White was 19 years old, he saw thousands of bats coming out of some caves. Jim explored the caves with a friend.

The two young spelunkers were amazed by what they saw in the caves. Minerals had been deposited by groundwater in shapes that looked like carrots on the floors and ceilings of the caves. Some of the shapes were gigantic. It must have taken thousands of years for the caves to form.

Jim told other people about his discovery. Scientists came to see and study the caves. The scientists said the underground caves were the largest they had ever seen. In 1930, the U.S. Government made the caves a national park called Carlsbad Caverns.

Many people visit Carlsbad Caverns National Park each year. A sign at the visitors' center honors Jim White. What a thrill it must have been to be one of the first people to see these famous caves! Maybe you have seen Carlsbad Caverns. If not, maybe you will someday.

Chapter Review

Summary

- Landforms are the features of the landscape.
- Some mountains are formed by volcanoes, faults, and folding.
- Corals are ocean animals that can form a coral reef.
- Groundwater can form caves.
- Rivers and glaciers make landforms by eroding and depositing Earth materials.
- Deposited sediments from floods can form a floodplain.
- Wind and waves can form sand dunes and beaches.
- Beaches are formed by waves.
- Piles of rock and soil are moved and deposited by glaciers.

Science Words

landforms	valleys	delta	sandbars
mountains	canyons	badlands	beach
coral reef	floodplain	sand dunes	moraines
caves			

Questions

1. List four landforms.
2. What mountains in the United States are folded mountains?
3. What landform is formed by faulting?
4. How were the Grand Tetons in Wyoming formed?
5. Where is a coral reef usually formed? Why?
6. How are caves and canyons different in the way they form?
7. How do floodplains form?
8. Describe how a delta is formed.
9. How are sandbars and sand dunes different?
10. What feature is formed by glaciers depositing Earth materials?

Self Checks

Answer these Self Checks on a sheet of paper.

1. Draw a diagram of the inside of the Earth and label the three different layers.

2. How do scientists know about the inside of the Earth if they have never been there?

3. What causes earthquakes and volcanoes?

4. In the picture, what evidence do you see for fast or slow change?

5. Name the agents of change at work in the above landscape.

6. How is the landscape above being changed by erosion and deposition?

7. Identify the landforms below. Which were made by erosion and which were made by deposition?

a   b

c

d

💡 Idea Corner
More Fun with Science

1. Build a model of the Earth. Show the crust, the mantle, and the core.

2. Learn about how scientists use seismographs. Write a story telling how a seismograph works.

3. Find a newspaper or magazine article about a fast change in the landscape. What caused the change? How did it affect the people who lived in the area? Give an oral report about the change.

4. Observe the school yard or vacant lot for evidence of erosion and deposition. How can you tell what caused erosion or deposition? Draw a top-view map of the area and show where erosion or deposition is located. Write a paragraph about how each may have been formed.

Reading for Fun

Earthquake! by John Gabriel Navarra, Doubleday and Company, Inc.: New York, © 1980.

Lots of photographs and diagrams will help you understand the causes of earthquakes and the efforts to predict them.

Glaciers: Nature's Frozen Rivers by Hershell H. Nixon and Joan Lowery Nixon, Dodd, Mead & Co.: New York, © 1980.

What about the glaciers of long ago? Where are glaciers today? Could it be that glaciers will be very useful to us in the future?

The Story of Geology: Our Changing Earth Through the Ages by Jerome Wyckoff, Western Golden Press: New York, © 1976.

Find out about the rocks and rock formations which make up the Earth's crust.

Unit 9

Plants in the Environment

Chapter One
Patterns in Plants

How are plants different? How are they alike?
What patterns can you find in plants? How can you
classify plants?

Imagine that your classroom is a beautiful forest. Pretend you are walking through the forest. Become aware of the properties in the plants around you. What do you see? How do the bark and leaves of the trees feel? How do the flowers smell? How many roots can you see?

Classifying Plants

There are many plants in the forest. You observe that some plants are different from others. How can you tell one plant from another? There are other living things that look like plants. How can you tell whether an object is a plant? Plants are living things that contain chlorophyll (KLOR uh fihl) and make their own food. What other properties of plants have you observed?

Scientists who study plants are called **botanists** (BAHT un usts). Botanists observe properties of plants. They look for similar properties or patterns. Recognizing patterns helps botanists classify plants. Patterns allow people to tell one plant group from another plant group. All the plants within a group are alike in some way. Each group has different patterns.

Activity

How Can You Classify Plants?

White pine

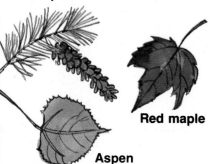

Red maple

Aspen

What to use:

leaves from different plants   pencil and paper
picture key

What to do:

1. Observe and note the properties of each leaf.

2. Look for similar properties or patterns in the leaves.

3. Group the leaves according to the patterns you observe.

4. Using the picture key, identify each leaf.

White oak

Sweet gum

Horse chestnut

Sycamore

Redwood

Coconut palm

What did you learn?

1. How are the leaves alike?
2. How are the leaves different?
3. What patterns did you use to group the leaves?
4. How can grouping and identifying leaves help you classify plants?

Using what you learned:

1. Why did you classify the leaves as you did?
2. Why do botanists classify plants in one way?

Two Plant Groups

Botanists classify plants into two large groups. Plants are either vascular (VAS kyuh lur) or nonvascular. **Vascular plants** are plants with tubes inside their leaves, stems, and roots. You may see tubes when you break or cut a stem. Water and food move through the tubes to all parts of the plants. **Nonvascular plants** are plants with no tubes inside them. Because of the tubes, vascular plants are considered more complex than nonvascular plants.

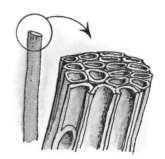

Nonvascular Plants

Mosses are one kind of nonvascular plant. **Mosses** are small plants with no true leaves, stems, or roots. Moss plants have parts that look like leaves, stems, and roots. However, the parts have no tubes to carry water through the plant. True leaves, stems, and roots have tubes. In mosses, water moves from cell to cell in the same way water is absorbed by a paper towel. Mosses must live where there is plenty of moisture. Why do you think mosses do not grow tall?

Mosses grow from spores. **Spores** are special cells that can grow into new plants. Spore cases which contain spores form at the top of a moss plant. When the spore cases burst open, some spores fall to the ground. Other spores may be blown long distances by the wind. If the spores fall in a moist, fertile place, new mosses may grow.

Moss plants grow in many places. Some mosses grow where it is warm and wet. Others grow where it is cold and the air is moist. You may have seen mosses growing on rocks or trees. They usually grow very close together. Some people think mosses look like a soft green carpet.

Vascular Plants

Most of the plants on Earth are vascular plants. Vascular plants have true roots, stems, and leaves. Since there are so many kinds of vascular plants, botanists classify them into smaller groups. The groups are vascular plants that do not produce seeds and vascular plants that do produce seeds.

Vascular Plants without Seeds

One group of vascular plants that does not produce seeds is **ferns.** Ferns are the simplest vascular plants. Ferns have roots, stems, and leaves. You may not see some fern stems because they are often underground. Only the leaves are seen. Most ferns have large, split leaves called **fronds** (FRAHNDZ). Some ferns lose the fronds in autumn. In spring, the new fronds may be curled up. As the fronds grow, they uncurl. Look at the frond shown here. Why do you think these curled fronds are called "fiddleheads"?

You may have seen rows of small brown bumps on the undersides of some fern leaves. The bumps are spore cases. When the cases burst open, spores fall to the ground. The spores grow into small, new plants that do not look like the adult ferns. The new plants produce special cells. When the special cells are joined together or fertilized, new fern plants grow. These look like the adult ferns. Although ferns produce spores like mosses, botanists consider ferns more complex than mosses. What makes ferns more complex than mosses?

You can find ferns growing almost anyplace on Earth. Some ferns grow on tree trunks. Others grow in lakes and ponds. A few ferns grow high on mountains where it is very cold. Ferns grow best in warm, shady places where the soil is damp and fertile. Ferns are most common in forests. Many people like to have ferns growing in and around their homes. The Boston fern is a popular houseplant.

Vascular Plants with Seeds

Most vascular plants produce seeds. Botanists consider vascular plants with seeds to be more complex than vascular plants without seeds. Seed plants have more complex parts than plants that do not produce seeds. Study the chart on pages 332 and 333. Notice how nonvascular and vascular plants are classified.

Seed plants are classified into two groups. One group is nonflowering plants. They form seeds without fruits. The second group is flowering plants. They form seeds in fruits.

Nonflowering Plants

Seed plants that do not produce seeds in fruits or flowers are nonflowering plants. Most of the nonflowering plants are conifers (KAHN uh furz). **Conifers** are plants that produce seeds in cones.

Many conifers are trees. Some are shrubs or vines. Maybe you have seen cones on pine trees. The cones of some conifers, such as juniper, look like berries. The seeds of conifers form inside the cones. Most conifers have needlelike leaves or scales.

Making Sure

1. How do vascular and nonvascular plants differ?
2. Are mosses vascular or nonvascular plants?
3. What groups of vascular plants produce seeds?

Flowering Plants

Flowering plants develop seeds from the flowers. Then fruits may develop from the flowers. Most of the plants we eat are flowering plants. Wildflowers, vegetable plants, grasses, and many trees are flowering plants. What are some other seed plants with flowers and fruits?

The flowering plant group can be divided into two smaller groups—monocots (MAHN uh kahtz) and dicots (DI kahtz). **Monocots** are flowering plants that produce seeds with one seed leaf. You can see the seed leaf in some monocots when the seed sprouts. In other monocots, the seed leaf stays below the ground when the seed sprouts. Most monocots are small plants such as lilies, wheat, and onions.

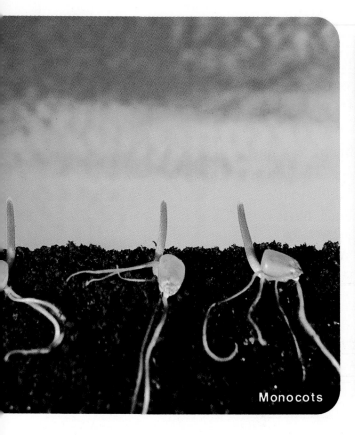

Monocots

Dicot

Dicots are flowering plants that produce seeds with two seed leaves. The seed leaves of some dicots also stay below the ground after the seed sprouts. Dicots include most flowers, vegetables, shrubs, and trees. What do "mono-" and "di-" mean?

 # Activity

How Can You Classify Flowering Plants Using Their Seeds?

What to use:

10 mixed seeds
2 flat pans (same size)
2 paper towels
hand lens

sprinkler bottle
water
pencil and paper

What to do:

1. Observe the seeds. Notice any likenesses or differences in them.

2. Cover the bottom of one flat pan with a paper towel. Use the sprinkler bottle and moisten the towel.

3. Place the ten mixed seeds on the damp towel. Cover the seeds with another damp paper towel and the other flat pan turned upside down. Keep the pans in a warm place.

4. Check the seeds each day for three weeks until the seeds begin to sprout. Be sure the paper towel is kept damp.

5. After each seed germinates, use a hand lens to observe it. Identify each plant as a monocot or a dicot.

6. Draw a picture of one monocot seedling and one dicot seedling. Label each seedling as a monocot or dicot.

What did you learn?

1. What likenesses or differences did you notice about the seeds before germination?
2. How can you identify monocot seedlings?
3. How can you identify dicot seedlings?
4. How many of your seeds are monocots?

Using what you learned:

1. If you observe a mature plant, how can you tell whether it is a monocot or a dicot?
2. Identify some common monocot and dicot plants. What differences can you name?

Monocots and dicots differ in other ways, too. In monocots, the tubes are scattered throughout the stem. In dicots, the tubes form a circle in the stem. Monocots have long, narrow leaves. Veins on the monocot leaves do not cross. Dicots have broad leaves. Veins on the dicot leaves are like the branches on a tree. Some veins branch out from one point and meet each other. Look at the leaves in the pictures above. Which plant is a monocot? How do you know?

Notice the flower petals on a monocot or dicot. Monocots can have three, six, or nine flower petals. Dicot flower petals appear in fours, fives, or a number divided evenly by four or five. Count the number of petals on the flowers in the pictures. Are they monocots or dicots?

Seed plants are an important part of our environment. Some roots, stems, leaves, seeds, and fruits are used as food by people. What parts of plants have you eaten today? Flowers may be used to make the environment more pleasant. Wood from seed plants is used to build chairs, tables, and desks. What other ways do people use wood?

Classifying Plants

A chart, or key, of the plant groups helps botanists classify plants. If you know the answers to five questions, you can classify any plant. Use the key below to classify plants.

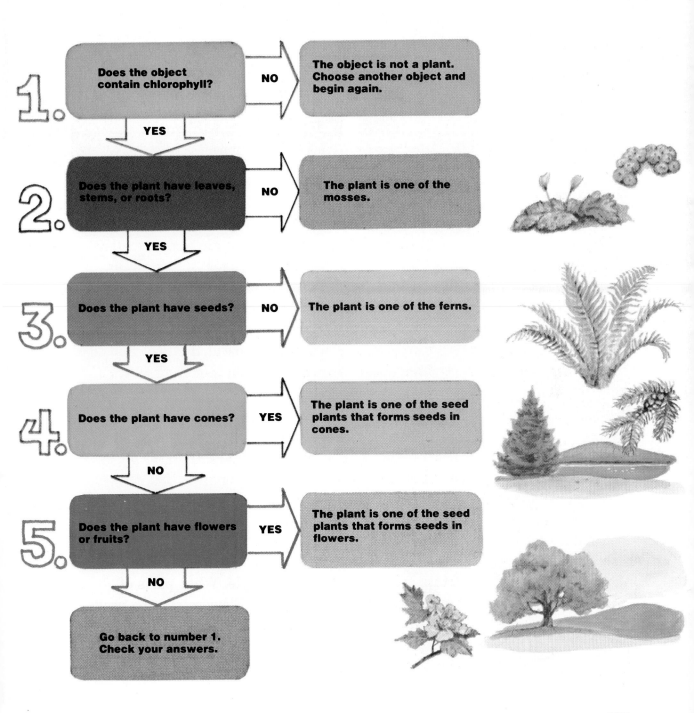

1. Does the object contain chlorophyll? → **NO** → The object is not a plant. Choose another object and begin again.

YES

2. Does the plant have leaves, stems, or roots? → **NO** → The plant is one of the mosses.

YES

3. Does the plant have seeds? → **NO** → The plant is one of the ferns.

YES

4. Does the plant have cones? → **YES** → The plant is one of the seed plants that forms seeds in cones.

NO

5. Does the plant have flowers or fruits? → **YES** → The plant is one of the seed plants that forms seeds in flowers.

NO

Go back to number 1. Check your answers.

331

Plant Classification

Nonvascular Plants

Mosses

Moss

Sphagnum moss

Spore cases

Spore cases

Spores

Vascular Plants

Nonflowering Plants

Ferns

Spore cases

Seeds

Conifers

Cones

Seeds

Flowering Plants

Monocots

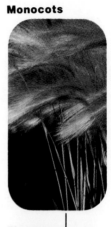

Flowers

Seeds

Dicots

Flowers

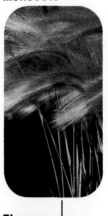

Save the Plants!

A giant cactus stands in an Arizona desert. It is over 15 meters tall and is very old. The giant cactus is a saguaro and grows in the foothills of northwestern Mexico, southwestern Arizona, and extreme southeastern California. Many years ago the Indians used the ribs of the saguaro for building huts and its fruit for food. Today the saguaro is one of thousands of plant species that is vanishing from the Earth. Why are plant species vanishing? Should we care if plants vanish? Can we do anything to save them?

Plants form the basis for all life on Earth. Some are useful as medicines. Some are used as food or shelter by animals. Many plants protect the Earth from the effects of erosion. Life on Earth would not exist if there were no plants.

Many people are becoming concerned about the great number of vanishing plant species and are working to save them. This may be done in several ways. The Garden Club of America has chosen to produce postcards about endangered or threatened plants. These postcards are an attempt to educate and encourage people to protect endangered plants and their habitats. The United States Congress passed the Endangered Species Act in 1973 to protect endangered and threatened wildlife and plants together with their habitats. A federal law in 1981 made it illegal to transport endangered animals or plants across state lines without approval of the state.

People are beginning to understand that each and every plant species on Earth is important. The extinction of plant species is a natural process, but people have sometimes increased the rate at which the process occurs. The positive steps being taken to halt the rapid process of extinction are encouraging. Perhaps, through human effort, the giant saguaro cactus will continue to grow for many more centuries in its native southwestern environment.

Chapter Review

Summary

- Plants are classified into two large groups—vascular and nonvascular.
- Nonvascular plants have no tubes to carry water and food.
- Vascular plants have tubes in their roots, stems, and leaves.
- Mosses are nonvascular plants with no true leaves, stems, or roots.
- Ferns are simple vascular plants.
- Conifers are nonflowering plants that produce seeds in cones.
- Flowering plants produce seeds from flowers.
- Monocots are flowering plants that have one seed leaf.
- Dicots are flowering plants that have two seed leaves.

Science Words

botanists	spores	conifers
vascular plants	ferns	monocots
nonvascular plants	fronds	dicots
mosses		

Questions

1. How are all plants alike?
2. Describe vascular and nonvascular plants.
3. What plants produce spores?
4. How do flowering and nonflowering seed plants differ?
5. What are the characteristics of conifers?
6. How do seed plants differ from ferns?
7. Describe the characteristics of monocots.
8. Describe the characteristics of dicots.
9. Name two monocot plants and two dicot plants.
10. Explain why flowering plants are the most complex plants.

Chapter Two

Plants Grow and Change

What kind of plants are these trees? How do you know whether the trees are alive or dead? How do you know whether the trees are young or old? How do plants change with time?

When is your birthday? Maybe you have seen pictures of yourself as a baby. How have you grown and changed since you were born? You will grow and change again in the next year. How old will you be next year? Your birth and growth are part of your life cycle.

What Is a Life Cycle?

You know what life means, but what does the word cycle mean? Cycles are actions that happen in the same order again and again. You are part of a life cycle. All living organisms have life cycles. Plants have life cycles. A **plant life cycle** includes its germination, growth, production of new plants, and death. This happens over and over again.

A flowering plant grows, blooms, produces seeds, and dies. The life cycle will be repeated when the new seeds from the plants germinate and grow. Different kinds of plants have different life cycles.

337

How Long Are Plant Life Cycles?

Some plants live through short life cycles. Tomato plants have short life cycles. They begin their life cycles as seeds in the early spring. Tomato plants grow and change during the spring, summer, and early fall. They produce small yellow flowers. Slowly, green fruits develop as the flowers die. Small seeds are forming inside the fruits. As the tomato fruits ripen, the seeds mature. Perhaps you have eaten the ripe fruit of the tomato plant. You may have observed the small yellow seeds inside the fruit. Cold autumn temperatures kill the tomato plants. Some people save the seeds to plant the next spring. The seeds start a new plant life cycle.

Tomato plants are annuals. **Annuals** (AN yulz) are plants that begin as seeds, grow, and die within one year or one growing season. Annuals have short life cycles. Some annuals complete their life cycles in only a few weeks. Corn, wheat, beans, marigolds, and zinnias (ZIHN ee uz) are annuals.

Other plants are called biennials (bi EN ee ulz). **Biennials** are plants that complete their life cycles in two years or two growing seasons. During the first year or growing season, biennials begin to grow and change. They grow roots, stems, and leaves. During the second year, biennials grow flowers and form fruits and seeds. The plant dies after the second year. Beets, carrots, turnips, and hollyhocks are examples of biennials. The biennials on the right are hollyhocks. In which year of their cycle are they?

Annuals

338

Biennials

Some plants have longer life cycles than annuals or biennials. Tulips are one example. Tulips grow from bulbs and bloom in the spring. The plants stay green for a few months. Then the leaves turn brown and die. However, the tulip bulbs stay alive underground. Next spring, new tulip plants will grow from the bulbs. Parts of the tulip life cycle will repeat for many years. Tulips are perennials (puh REN ee ulz).

Perennials are plants that live more than two years before completing a life cycle. Not all perennial plants have bulbs. Some perennials like peonies (PEE uh neez), daisies, violets, and lilies lose their leaves and stems each year. The roots remain alive in the ground. Other perennials with hard, woody stems lose only their leaves each autumn. Which perennials have stems visible all year?

Trees are perennials with long life cycles. Most trees live for many years. You may think a tree will live forever. Some Sequoia trees are over 4000 years old. Yet, trees are living things with a beginning time, growing time, and dying time. At the end of their life cycles, trees die, too. In what part of the life cycle do you see most trees?

The Life of a Tree

Perhaps you or some of your friends have kept a diary or daily record of your lives. There is a record, like a diary, inside every tree. A new wood layer grows on the trunk each year. Each layer, or **annual ring,** shows one year or season of growth. The annual rings of a tree can indicate events in the life of a tree.

Narrow annual rings may mean years of dry weather with very little growth. Wide annual rings are signs of wet weather with much growth. Find the age of a tree by counting the number of annual rings. How old is this tree? Which years did the tree grow best? Which years had dry weather? A scar on an annual ring shows injury to the tree that year.

The injury may have been caused by a forest fire or from a falling tree limb. Carving into the bark can also cause injury to a tree. Injuries to the stem may cause the tree to become diseased.

How Do Plants Grow?

All cells need food for growth. Certain plant cells are able to make food by photosynthesis. Light, carbon dioxide, and water are needed for photosynthesis. What will happen if plants do not have light, air, and water?

Chlorophyll is a chemical in plant cells that makes photosynthesis possible. The green-colored chlorophyll absorbs light. Without chlorophyll, plants could not use light to make food.

Carbon dioxide in air enters a leaf through small openings called **stomata** (STOH mut uh). Stomata are pores through which carbon dioxide is taken in and oxygen is released. Plant roots absorb water and minerals from the soil. When a plant has light, carbon dioxide, and water, it can make food by photosynthesis. Photosynthesis takes place in leaves and other green parts of a plant.

Light affects photosynthesis. In summer, more photosynthesis takes place than in winter because there is more light. More plant growth also occurs in summer. Why do you think less plant growth occurs in winter?

Making Sure

1. What is the life cycle of a plant?
2. How is a perennial different from an annual?
3. What is necessary for photosynthesis?

Plants and the Seasons

Plant growth changes with the seasons. Autumn has fewer hours of sunlight, so less photosynthesis takes place then. What plant growth change do you notice in autumn?

Plants that lose their leaves in autumn are called **deciduous** (dih SIHJ uh wus) **plants.** In the winter deciduous plants might seem dead, but they are not. The plant growth is slower.

Look at the deciduous trees pictured here. Find the picture where you think the most amount of photosynthesis is occurring. What season is it? Trees use some of the food produced in photosynthesis for growth. Some food is also stored in the roots. At what time of the year would the stored food be used? Find the picture of the trees where you think the least amount of photosynthesis is occurring. What season is it?

Photosynthesis takes place all year in evergreens. **Evergreens** are plants that stay green all year. Pine trees, cedars, and redwoods are evergreen plants. Shrubs such as holly and rhododendron are also evergreens. Some evergreens have needlelike leaves. Evergreens keep their leaves throughout the year. A few needles are lost from the plants during each season. However, the fallen needles are replaced by new needles.

Activity

How Are Light and Water Important to Plant Growth?

What to use:

4 green plants in pots   masking tape
crayon or marker   pencil and paper

What to do:

1. Use a crayon to mark small pieces of masking tape for each plant pot. Number the pots 1, 2, 3, and 4.

2. Place pots 1 and 2 in a sunny spot.

3. Place pots 3 and 4 in a dark closet.

4. Water plants 1 and 3 as needed. Do not water plants 2 and 4.

5. Observe the plants daily for 2 weeks. Record your observations on a chart each day.

What did you learn?

1. What differences do you observe between plants 1 and 3?

2. What differences do you observe between plants 2 and 4?

3. Why do you think some plants grow better than others?

Using what you learned:

1. What would help plants 2, 3, and 4 grow better?

2. What factors are necessary for good plant growth?

3. What would happen if a plant had light and water but no air? Try it for 2 weeks. Water a plant and put petroleum jelly on both sides of several leaves. Water it again if necessary.

People and Science

Plans and Plants

City planners are people who design communities. They make master plans of a community as they think it should be. City planners try to make cities pleasant places to live. Do you find a forest or a city more pleasant? City planners try to include a little bit of the forest in cities.

One of the ways city planners make cities more pleasant is with plants. In master plans, the city planner includes plants for many purposes. City planners experiment with plants that grow best on roadsides. There the soil is often dry and the air is polluted. It is important that city planners know which plants will grow best in these conditions.

Grass may be planted in cities to make soft green walkways for people. Trees are planted along the sides of roads to shield people from traffic pollution. Evergreens help reduce road noise. Trees help purify air that is polluted by automobile fumes. Flowers also help make the air smell nice. What flowers smell nice to you? What are some sounds that you like to hear? Some birds and other animals will come to live in the plants of cities. Then we may hear some of the pleasant sounds of the forest in the city.

Chapter Review

Summary

- The life cycle of a plant includes its germination, growth, production of new plants, and death.
- Annuals begin, grow, and die within one year.
- Biennials begin, grow, and die in two years.
- Perennials repeat phases of their life cycles and live for more than two years.
- Plants make their own food by photosynthesis.
- Annual rings in trees show one year or season of growth.
- Stomata are small openings in leaves and stems through which air enters and leaves the plant.
- Plants that lose their leaves in autumn are deciduous.
- Plants that remain green all year are evergreens.

Science Words

plant life cycle	biennials	annual ring	deciduous plants
annuals	perennials	stomata	evergreens

Questions

1. How can you tell in what stage of the life cycle a rose bush is if it has flower buds?
2. Tell how the life cycles of annuals and biennials differ.
3. Name three annuals.
4. Name three perennials.
5. How do biennials and perennials differ?
6. How are stomata important in photosynthesis?
7. Why is photosynthesis important in green plants?
8. Why do some leaves change color in autumn?
9. What group of plants lose their leaves in fall and winter?
10. What group of plants stay green all year?

Self Checks

Answer these Self Checks on a sheet of paper.

1. Name two ways that seed plants form seeds.
2. How are mosses and ferns different?
3. In what ways are mosses and seed plants alike?
4. Why is chlorophyll important to plants?
5. Why is photosynthesis necessary for plant growth?
6. Describe a plant life cycle.
7. Explain the difference between annuals and perennials.
8. What can you learn from observing the annual rings of a tree?
9. Explain the life cycle of a biennial plant.
10. How would you classify the plants shown?

Idea Corner
More Fun with Science

1. Find out how to make a terrarium. Plant some seed plants, ferns, and mosses in your terrarium.
2. Classify the plants growing inside and around your home. Try to find out which ones are annuals and which ones are perennials.
3. Make a list of all the plants you eat for food. Separate the foods into groups of seeds, stems, roots, leaves, and flowers.
4. Take a walk through a forest. Try to find a plant from each plant group. Make a drawing of the plants you find and where you find them growing.
5. Design an experiment to test how the direction of light affects plant growth.

Reading for Fun

Seasons of the Tallgrass Prairie by Carol Lerner, William Morrow and Company: New York, © 1980.
  A great visual and written description of prairie plant life through the seasons.

The Gentle Desert: Exploring an Ecosystem by Lawrence Pringle, Macmillan Publishing Company: New York, © 1977.
  There is much more to a desert than sand. Read how plants survive in a desert.

A Walk in the Forest: The Woodlands of North America by Albert List, Jr. and Ilka List, Thomas Y. Crowell: New York, © 1977.
  How do the plants and animals vary from forest to forest?

Glossary

This book has words that you may not have read before. Many of these words are science words. Some science words may be hard for you to read. You will find the science words in **bold print.** These words may appear two ways. The first way shows how the word is spelled. The second way shows how the word

sounds. The lists below show the sounds each letter or group of letters make.

Look at the word **energy** (EN ur jee). The second spelling shows the letters "ee." Find these letters in the list. The "ee" has the sound of "ea" in the word "leaf." Anytime you see "ee" in the second spelling, you know what sound to say.

a . . . back (BAK)
er . . . care, fair (KER, FER)
ay . . . day (DAY)
ah . . . father (FAHTH ur)
ar . . . car (KAR)
ow . . . flower, loud (FLOW ur, LOWD)
e . . . less (LES)
ee . . . leaf (LEEF)
ih . . . trip (TRIHP)
i(i+con+e) . . .
   idea, life (i DEE uh, LIFE)
oh . . . go (GOH)
aw . . . soft (SAWFT)
or . . . orbit (OR but)
oy . . . coin (KOYN)

oo . . . foot (FOOT)
yoo . . . pure (PYOOR)
ew . . . food (FEWD)
yew . . . few (FYEW)
uh(u+con) . . .
   comma, mother (KAHM uh, MUTH ur)
sh . . . shelf (SHELF)
ch . . . nature (NAY chur)
g . . . gift (GIHFT)
j . . . gem, edge (JEM, EJ)
ing . . . sing (SING)
zh . . . vision (VIHZH un)
k . . . cake (KAYK)
s . . . seed, cent (SEED, SENT)
z . . . zone, raise (ZOHN, RAYZ)

A

acceleration (ihk sel uh RAY shun): an increase in the speed of an object

agents of change: factors that change the landscape such as water, wind, and ice

air masses: large bodies of air that move across land and water

air pressure: the pressing down of the air on the Earth's surface

alcohol (AL kuh hawl): a drug that slows down the nervous system

amphibians (am FIHB ee unz): cold-blooded vertebrates that live part of their lives in water and part of their lives on land

anemometer (an uh MAHM ut ur): instrument for measuring wind speed

annual ring: a layer of wood on a tree trunk showing one year or one season of growth

annuals (AN yulz): plants that begin as seeds, grow, make new plants, and die in one year or growing season

arthropods (AR thruh pahdz): animals with outer skeletons, jointed legs, and segmented bodies

astronomers (uh STRAN uh murz): scientists who study the stars

astronomical (as tru NAM ih kul) **unit:** the distance from the Earth to the sun

atmosphere (AT muh sfihr): a blanket of air surrounding the Earth

atoms (AT umz): the building blocks of all matter; tiny particles

B

badlands: landforms caused by erosion and marked by hills and valleys with unusual shapes

barometer (buh RAHM ut ur): an instrument that measures air pressure

beach: eroded rock or deposited sand along a shore

bearing: a round, smooth object that can reduce friction between two surfaces

Beaufort scale (BOH furt·SKAYL): a scale that shows numbers for wind speed

biennials (bi EN ee ulz): plants that begin, grow, make new plants, and die within two years or two growing seasons

Big Dipper: a constellation that looks like a large dipper

birds: vertebrates with feathers for a body covering

body covering system: the skin, hair, and nails

boiling point: the temperature at which a liquid has gained enough heat energy to change to a gas

bones: hard structures made of living cells and minerals

botanists (BAHT un usts): scientists who study plants

brain: the main control center of the body and the nervous system

C

caffeine: a drug that will speed up the nervous system

calcium (KAL see um): one of the minerals that makes bones hard

canyons (KAN yunz): deep valleys with steep sides

cardiac (KAHRD ee ak) **muscle:** the heart muscle

cartilage (KART ul ihj): a firm, flexible substance that forms parts of some skeletons

caves: large, empty spaces in the ground made by groundwater erosion

cerebellum (ser uh BEL um): the part of the brain that controls the voluntary muscles of the body

cerebrum (suh REE brum): the part of the brain that controls your ability to think, learn, and talk

chemical (KEM ih kul) **energy:** energy stored in molecules of matter

cirrus (SIHR us) **clouds:** thin, white clouds with featherlike edges

classifying (KLAS uh fy ing): grouping by likenesses or differences

climate (KLI mut): the average weather of an area for many years

cold-blooded animals: animals having a body temperature the same as their environment

compounds (KAHM powndz): matter made up of more than one kind of element

conclusion (kun KLEW zhun): a decision or answer to a problem or question

condensation (kahn den SAY shun): the change of a gas to a liquid when heat energy is lost

conduction (kun DUK shun): the transfer of heat energy by direct contact of source and receiver

conifers (KAHN uh furz): plants that produce seeds in cones

conserving (kun SURV ing): saving or not wasting

constellation (kahn stuh LAY shun): a star group with a definite pattern

contracted (kun TRAKT ud) **muscle:** a muscle that becomes tighter and shorter

convection (kun VEK shun): the transfer of heat energy by the movement of heated gases or liquids

coral reef: a landform made by thousands of coral coverings

core: the ball-shaped center of the Earth

crust: the outer or top layer of the Earth

crystals (KRIHS tulz): particles with a fixed shape that occur in a repeating order in solids

cube: an object whose length, width, and height have the same measurement

cumulus (KYEW myuh lus) **clouds:** clouds that appear large, thick, and puffy

D

daily mean: the average temperature for a day

deceleration (dee sel uh RAY shun): a decrease in the speed of an object

deciduous (dih SIHJ uh wus) **plants:** plants that lose their leaves in autumn

delta (DEL tuh): a fan-shaped landform made of sediments from suddenly slowed moving water

density (DEN sut ee): the amount of mass an object has for its volume

deposition (dep uh ZISH un): the dropping or laying down of rocks and soil by agents of change

dermis (DUR muhs): the inner layer of skin below the epidermis

dicots (DI kahtz): flowering plants that produce seeds containing two seed leaves

direct observation (di REKT· ahb sur VAY shun): both sensing and measuring the properties of matter

drugs: chemicals that cause a change in the nervous system and other systems of the body

dwarf stars: stars that are smaller in mass than our sun

E

earthquakes: movements of large areas of the Earth's crust caused by changes below the surface

electric energy: energy due to the charged particles of matter

electric force: the push or pull of electric charges on objects

element (EL uh munt): matter made of all the same kind of atoms

elliptical (ih LIHP tih kuhl) **galaxies:** galaxies that are oval in shape with a definite pattern of stars

energy (EN ur jee): ability to do work

energy chain: the transfer and change of energy from one form to another form

energy receiver: a person or object receiving energy

energy source: a person or object that gives off energy

energy transfer (TRANS fur): the flow of energy from a source to a receiver

epidermis (ep uh DUR mus): the outer or top layer of skin that you can see

erosion (ih ROH zhun): the carrying away of rocks and soil by agents of change

evaporation (ih vap uh RAY shun): the change of a liquid to a gas

evergreens: plants that stay green all year

experiment (ihk SPER uh munt): a test that provides information to solve a problem or answer a question

F

fault (FAHLT): a break in the Earth's crust along which rock layers move due to changes in pressure below the surface

ferns: plants with tubes in the leaves, stems, and roots that reproduce by spores

first law of motion: a law that states objects at rest stay at rest and objects in motion stay in motion unless acted on by a force

fish: the simplest group of vertebrates having scales, fins, and gills

floodplain: the flat valley bottom along a river

force: a push or a pull

forecast (FOR kast): a prediction of what the weather will be

fracture (FRAK chur): a crack or a break in a bone

freezing point: the temperature at which a liquid becomes a solid

friction (FRIHK shun): a force that slows down or stops moving objects

fronds (FRAHNDZ): the large, split leaves of ferns

front: the place where two air masses meet

G

galaxy (GAL uhk see): a large group of stars, gas, and dust

giant stars: stars that are larger in mass than our sun

gills: organs through which fish get oxygen from the water

glands (GLANDZ): special groups of cells that produce and store substances

grams (GRAMZ): a unit of mass

gravity (GRAV ut ee): the pulling force of every object on all other objects

groundwater: water trapped in soil and rock spaces, an agent of change

H

heat energy: the energy from the movement of particles that make up a substance

hollow-bodied animals: invertebrates with a hollow center and only one opening

humidity (hyew MIHD ut ee): water vapor in the air

hurricanes (HUR uh kayhnz): storms with strong winds and heavy rains; occur over a long time and a large area

I

indirect observation (ihn di REKT·ahb sur VAY shun): does not allow us to make direct measurements or use all our senses

insulation (ihn suh LAY shun): a substance that reduces the transfer of heat

invertebrates (in VURT uh brayts): animals without backbones

involuntary muscles (ihn VAHL un ter ee·MUS ulz): work or move on their own

irregular galaxies: galaxies that do not have a special shape or form

J

joints: places where bones are joined together

joule (JEWL): a unit of work equal to a newton-meter

K

kilograms (KIHL uh gramz): one thousand grams

kinetic (kuh NET ihk) **energy:** the energy of any object in motion

L

landforms: features of the landscape including mountains, valleys, beaches, and plains

landscape: a part of the Earth's surface that you can see

ligaments (LIHG uh munts): strong, tough fibers that hold bones together at the joints

light energy: visible radiant energy that can travel through space and some matter

light-year: the distance light travels in one year

Little Dipper: a constellation that looks like a dipper; smaller than the Big Dipper

lubricants (LEW brih kunts): substances that make surfaces smooth and slippery

M

magnetic field: the area of force around magnets

mammals: vertebrates with fur or hair; females can produce milk for their young

mantle (MANT uhl): a layer of Earth consisting of mostly rock, under the crust

mass (MAS): the amount of matter in an object

matter (MAT ur): a solid, liquid, or gas that takes up space

mechanical advantage: the amount that a machine can increase a force

mechanical (mih KAN ih kul) **energy:** energy due to the position or motion of people or objects

medulla (muh DUL uh): the bottom part of the brain that controls some involuntary muscles

melting point: the temperature at which a solid becomes a liquid

meteorologists (meet ee uh RAHL uh justs): scientists who study weather

model (MAHD ul): may be used to explain what cannot be directly observed

molecules (MAHL ih kyewlz): two or more atoms joined together in a certain way

mollusks (MAHL usks): invertebrates with soft bodies; many have shells

molting (MOHLT ing): the shedding of the outer skeleton

monocots (MAHN uh kahtz): flowering plants that produce seeds containing one seed leaf

moraines (muh RAYNS): ridges of long, low piles of rock and soil deposited by glaciers

mosses: nonvascular plants without true leaves, stems, or roots

motion: changing position; occurs as result of a push or pull

motor (MOHT ur) **nerves:** nerves that carry messages from the brain to the muscles

mountains: sections of the Earth's crust that are higher than nearby areas

muscles (MUS ulz): special tissues that move body parts

N

nerves (NURVZ): threadlike cells throughout the body that carry messages to and from the brain

nervous (NUR vus) **system:** the brain, spinal cord, and nerves

newtons (NEWT unz): the unit for measuring weight

nicotine (NIHK uh teen): a drug found in tobacco that acts to speed up the nervous system

nonvascular (nahn VAS kyuh lur) **plants:** plants without tubes inside the leaves, stems, and roots

P

parasites (PER uh sites): living things that feed on other living things

perennials (puh REN ee ulz): plants that live more than two years or two seasons before completing a life cycle

petroleum (puh TROL ee um): a thick liquid used as the basis of gasoline; crude oil

pigment (PIHG munt): a substance in the dermis that gives color to the skin

plant life cycle: includes its germination, growth, production of new plants, and death; occurs again and again

Polaris (puh LER us): the star located directly above the Earth's north pole; the North Star

pores (POHRZ): small openings in the skin

position: the place where you are or where an object is

potential (puh TEN chul) **energy:** energy that is stored

precipitation: water returning to the Earth's surface from the atmosphere

prediction (prih DIHKT shun): a guess of what you think may happen

pressure (PRESH ur): a measure of the force applied to a certain area

properties (PRAHP urt eez): what we can sense or measure

R

radar (RAY dar): a method used to locate objects or precipitation using radio waves

radiant (RAYD ee unt) **energy:** a form of energy that travels in waves

radiation (rayd ee AY shun): the transfer of energy by waves

reflex (REE fleks): a special body action involving only nerves and spinal cord

regenerate (rih JEN uh rayt): regrowing of missing body parts

relative humidity: a comparison of water vapor present in air to the amount of water vapor air can hold

relaxed muscle: one which is looser and longer than a contracted muscle

reptiles (REP tilez): vertebrates that have dry, scaly skin

Richter (RIHK tur) **scale:** series of numbers from 0 to 10 used to compare the force of earthquakes

S

sandbars: piles of sand and rock deposited by moving water

sand dunes: large hills formed of windblown sand

scales: thin, smooth pieces of a bonelike material that cover the entire body of the fish

scavengers (SKAV un jurz): animals that eat dead animals

scientific method (si un TIHF ihk· METH ud): the way scientists solve problems or find answers to questions

second law of motion: an object's acceleration depends on the mass of the object and the size and direction of the force acting on it

sediments (SED uh munts): earth materials deposited by agents of change

seismographs (SIZE muh grafs): instruments that measure the force of earthquake shock waves

sensory (SENS uh ree) **nerves:** nerves that carry a message from a body part to the brain

Sirius (SIHR ee uhs): the brightest star seen from the northern hemisphere; found in the constellation Canis Major

skeletal muscles (SKEL uh tuhl· MUS ulz): muscles surrounding the bones, allowing you to move your bones

skeleton: a structure that gives shape, supports, and protects an animal's body

skin: the outer part of the body covering system

skull: bones that surround the brain; gives shape to the head

smooth muscles: the involuntary muscles of the body organs

solar (SOH lar) **energy:** radiant energy from the sun

speed: a measure of how fast an object moves

spinal (SPIN ul) **cord:** a thick, cordlike bundle of nerve cells along which messages travel

spiny-skinned animals (SPI nee- SKIND·AN uh muhls): invertebrate animals that have sharp spines on the outsides of their bodies

spiral galaxies: galaxies that have spiral or curved arms

sponges: the simplest invertebrates

spores (SPOHRZ): special cells from mosses or ferns that grow into new mosses or ferns

sprain (SPRAYN): a condition that occurs when ligaments tear or stretch away from the bones

stomata (STOH mut uh): small openings in a leaf through which carbon dioxide enters and oxygen is released

stratus clouds: thick layers of clouds that form a blanket over the land

T

tendons (TEN dunz): tough white tissues that attach muscles to bones

thermostats (THUR muh stats): switches that control heating and cooling systems

third law of motion: for every action force, there is an equal and opposite reaction force

thunderstorms: strong, local storms with lightning and thunder

tornado (tor NAYD oh): a very strong windstorm; funnel-shaped

troposphere (TROHP uh sfihr): the part of the atmosphere closest to the Earth's surface

V

valleys: low areas usually formed between mountains

vascular (VAS kyuh lur) **plants:** plants with tubes in their leaves, stems, and roots

vertebrates (VURT uh brayts): animals with backbones

volcanoes (vahl KAY nohz): openings in the Earth's crust through which magma and gases flow

volume (VAHL yum): the amount of space matter takes up

voluntary muscles (VAHL un ter ee · MUS ulz): move when you control or direct them

W

warm-blooded animals: animals that have an unchanging body temperature

weathering (WETH uh ring): breaking of rocks into smaller pieces by the agents of change

weight: the measure of the amount of pull or gravity between objects

work: the result of a force that causes a motion; work = force × distance an object moves

worms: soft-bodied invertebrates that are classified into three groups: flat, round, or segmented

X

X rays: radiant energy that can pass through liquids, gases, and some solids

Z

zodiac: the path the sun follows

Index

heat, 239, 249–251
kinetic energy, 234
light, 240
mechanical, 237
potential, 235
radiant, 240–242
radio waves, 242
receiver, 245
solar, 241
source, 245
transfer, 246
transportation, 268
X rays, 241
Energy chain, 254
Epidermis, 117–118
Erosion, 291
Evaporation, 72
Evergreens, 342
Exercise, 144
Experiment, 42

F

Fault, 282–283
Ferns, 325
Fish, 7–10
Flood plain, 307–308
Floods, 296–297
Flowering plants, 327–328
  dicots, 328
  monocots, 327
Flowers
  annuals, 338
  biennials, 338–339
  perennials, 339
Force, 161, 168–169
  electric, 177
  friction, 173–175, 194
  gravity, 162, 178–179
  magnetic, 176
Forecast, 97
Fracture, 133–134
  compound, 134
  simple, 134

Freezing point, 76
Friction, 173–175, 194, 253
Fronds, 325
Front, 100
Fuel, 260

G

Galaxies, 207–211
  elliptical, 211
  irregular, 211
  spiral, 211
  types of, 210–211
Gas, 73–76
Geologists, 280–281
Giant stars, 206
Glaciers, 297
Glands, 118
Grams, 55
Gravity, 162, 178–179
Groundwater, 296
Groups
  of animals, 7

H

Hair, 122–123
Healthy bones, 129
Heat energy, 239, 249–251
Heating, 260–261
Hollow-bodied animals, 25–26
Humidity, 92
Hurricanes, 104

I

Igneous rock, 280
Indirect observation, 44
Insulation, 263
Invertebrates, 6, 23
  arthropods, 31–32
  hollow-bodied animals, 25–26

mollusks, 28–30
spiny-skinned animals, 34
sponges, 24–25
worms, 27–28
Irregular galaxies, 211

J

Jellyfish, 25–26
Joints, 131
ball and socket, 131–132
fixed, 131
hinge, 132
pivot, 132

K

Kilograms, 55
Kinetic energy, 234

L

Landforms, 301
badlands, 308
beach, 312
canyons, 306
caves, 306
coral reef, 305
delta, 308
floodplain, 307–308
moraines, 313
mountains, 301–302, 304
sandbars, 310
sand dunes, 309
valleys, 306
volcanoes, 281–282
Landscape, 289
agents of change, 291
Ligaments, 133
Light energy, 240

Light-year, 204
Liquids, 69–72
Little Dipper, 219
Lubricants, 196

M

Machines, 190–193
bearings, 196
lubricants, 196
Magnetic field, 176
Mammals, 17–20
Mantle, 280–281
Mass, 55
Matter, 41
compounds, 48–52
density of, 62
elements, 47–48
gas, 73–76
liquids, 69–70
properties of, 55
solids, 67–69
Mechanical energy, 237
Medulla, 148
Melting point, 68
Metallurgists, 64
Metals, 48
Metamorphic rock, 280
Meteorologists, 97
Milky Way galaxy, 207–208
Model, 44
Molecules, 46
Mollusks, 28–30
Monocots, 327
Moraines, 313
Mosses, 323–325
Motion, 161
laws of, 162, 166, 169
Motor nerves, 150
Mountains, 301–302, 304
Muscles, 137
cardiac, 138
care of, 142–143
contracted, 141

Solar energy, 241
Solids, 67–69
Speed, 163
Spine, 128
Spiny-skinned animals, 34
Spiral galaxies, 211
Sponges, 24–25
Spores, 324
Sprain, 133
Stars
    Alpha Centauri, 204
    Antares, 206
    brightness, 205
    colors of, 206–207
    constellation, 215, 217–225
    dwarf, 206
    galaxies, 207–211
    giant, 206
    Polaris, 218–219
Stomata, 341
Storms, 101–104
    hurricanes, 104
    thunderstorms, 101
    tornadoes, 101
Stratus clouds, 93
Summer solstice, 226
Sun, 208

T

Tendons, 139
Thermogram, 256
Thermophotographer, 256
Thermostats, 262
Thunderstorms, 101
Tornadoes, 101
Transfer of energy, 246
    conduction, 249
    convection, 249
    radiation, 250
Transportation, 268
Trees, 340–341

V

Valleys, 306
Vascular plants, 323, 324–327
Vertebrates, 6
    amphibians, 11–12
    birds, 14–17
    fish, 7–10
    mammals, 17–20
    reptiles, 12–13
Volcanoes, 281–282
Volume, 60

W

Warm-blooded animals
    birds, 14–17
    mammals, 17–20
Waves, 297
Weather, 93
    air masses, 99–100
    climate, 105–107
    front, 100
    storms, 101–104
Weather forecasters, 242
Weathering, 291
Weight, 57–59
Wind, 298
Wind vane, 89
Winter storm, 102–103
Work, 187
    formula for, 188
Worms, 27–28

X

X rays, 241

Z

Zodiac, 225

PHOTO CREDITS

2, 3, E.R. Degginger/Bruce Coleman; **4,** Tom Carroll/FPG; **5,** Animals Animals; **6,** Carl Roessler/Bruce Coleman; **7,** Richard Brommer; **8** (t) Doug Martin, (m) Joey Jacques, (b) Russ Lappa; **9** (tl) Roger K. Burnard, (tr) Ken Weskrslcon/FPG, (bl)(br) Tom Stack/Tom Stack & Associates; **10** (l) T.F.H. Publications, H.J. Richter, (r) Sam Zook, Jr.; **11** (tr)(br) Al Staffan, (mr) David M. Dennis, (bl) Gene Frazier; **12,** Al Nelson/Tom Stack & Associates; **13** (tl) Michael Collier, (tr)(br) Al Staffan; **14** (t)(m) Al Staffan, (b) Bob McKeever/Tom Stack & Associates; **16** (tl) Bill & Joan Popejoy, (m)(bl) Al Staffan, (br) Animals Animals/© G.L. Kooyman; **17** (t) Gary Milburn/Tom Stack & Associates, (m) Al Staffan, (b) Animals Animals/© Leonard Lee Rue III; **18** (tl) Al Staffan, (tr) Roger K. Burnard, (b) Larry Hamill; **19** (t) Bill & Joan Popejoy, (m) Richard Alley, (b) Al Staffan; **20** (l) Cliff Beaver, (r) Beattie/FPG; **22,** Al Staffan; **23,** Roger K. Burnard; **24** (l) Tom Stack/Tom Stack & Associates, (r) Richard Brommer; **25** (t) Howard Hall/Tom Stack & Associates, (bl) Tom Stack/Tom Stack & Associates, (br) David G. Wacker/Tom Stack & Associates; **26,** R.G. Bachand; **27** (t) David M. Dennis, (b) Em Ahart/Tom Stack & Associates; **28, 29,** Al Staffan; **31** (t) Gene Frazier, (m) Al Staffan, (b) Tom Stack/Tom Stack & Associates; **32** (l) Gene Frazier, (r) Robert Fridenstine, (c) Roger K. Burnard, (b) Animals Animals/© Zig Leszczynski; **33,** Ted Rice; **34** (t) Ruth Dixon, (m) Gerald A. Corsi/Tom Stack & Associates, (b) Gene Frazier; **36** (tl) Tom Stack/Tom Stack & Associates, (tm)(bl) Al Staffan, (tr) Al Nelson/Tom Stack & Associates, (br) Roger K. Burnard; **38, 39,** Roger K. Burnard; **40,** Larry Hamill; **42,** James Westwater; **44** (t) Doug Martin, (b) National Highway Traffic Safety Administration; **46,** Greg Miller; **47,** Lightforce; **48** (tm) Smithsonian Institute, (t) Rick Kocks, (bl) Robert Shay; **49,** James Westwater; **52** (bl) Lightforce, (br) Greg Miller; **54,** Roger K. Burnard; **55,** Richard Brommer; **60** (t) Hickson-Bender Photography, (b) Roger K. Burnard; **61,** Petland Marion/Hickson-Bender Photography; **62** (t) Studio Productions, (b) Don Nieman; **64,** George Hunter/FPG; **66,** Bill & Joan Popejoy; **67,** Roger K. Burnard; **68,** Larry Hamill; **69** (t) David M. Dennis, (b) Larry Hamill; **75,** Richard Brommer; **78** (tl) Tom Stack/Tom Stack & Associates, (tr) Wayne Feamster, (bl) Bill & Joan Popejoy, (br) Steve Bogen; **80, 81,** Animals Animals/© Fran Allen; **82,** James Westwater; **83,** Paul Brown; **85,** Hickson-Bender Photography; **86** (tl)(tr) Michele Wigginton, (bl)(br) Phil Feldmeier; **87,** Latent Image; **88** (l) Craig Kramer, (r) Don Parsisson; **89** (tl) Larry Hamill, (tr) Ad Image Photography, (bl) Robert Ault, Marion Municipal Airport/Hickson-Bender Photography, (br) Paul Brown; **92** (l) Wayne Scherr/Tom Stack & Associates, (r) Tom Stack/Tom Stack & Associates; **93** (l) Roger K. Burnard, (r) Bill & Joan Popejoy; **94,** David R. Frazier; **96,** Bill & Joan Popejoy; **97,** Paul Brown; **101** (r) Bob Hamburgh/Tom Stack & Associates, (l) Myles Willard/Tom Stack & Associates; **104,** Harry Palmer; **105,** Bill & Joan Popejoy; **106** (l) Susan Rhoades, (r) Phil Feldmeier; **107** (l) Keith Gunnar/Tom Stack & Associates, (r) Nick Anspach; **112** (tl)(bl) Paul Brown, (tr) Ad Image Photography, (br) Bruce Sampsel; **114, 115** George Anderson/ICOM; **116,** James Westwater; **117, 119, 121,** George Anderson/ICOM; **122** (t) Studio Productions, (m) Rick Kocks, (bl) Strix Pix, (bm) Michael Collier, (br) Freda Leinwand; **123, 124,** File Photo; **126,** Roger K. Burnard; **127,** Bob & Miriam Francis/Tom Stack & Associates; **129,** Tim Courlas; **131,** George Anderson/ICOM; **134,** Tim Courlas; **136,** Larry Hamill; **142** (l) Paul Brown, (r) Frank Balthis; **143** (t) Steve Lissau, (bl) Breta Westlund/Tom Stack & Associates, (br) Bill & Joan Popejoy; **144,** J. Webber/Tom Stack & Associates; **146,** Dick Pietzrzyk/Tom Stack & Associates; **150,** Skip Comer/Latent Image; **153,** Gerard Photography; **154** (t) Robert Shay, (b) Studio Productions; **158, 159,** Steve Lissau; **160,** Doug Martin; **161,** Roger K. Burnard; **162,** Michael Collier; **163** (tr) Roger K. Burnard, (m) Rick Kocks; **166,** J.H. Meyer/Tom Stack & Associates; **168** (t) Six Flags Over Georgia, (bl)(br) George Anderson/ICOM; **169,** Skip Comer/Latent Image; **170,** George Anderson/ICOM; **172,** Bob Horne; **173** (tr) Roger K. Burnard, (bl) Wayne Feamster, (bm)(br) Michael Collier; **174** (t) Steve Lissau, (b) © David Scharf/Peter Arnold; **175** (r) Studio Ten, (l) Joseph DiChello, Jr.; **176** (r) Morgan Photos, (l) Gerard Photography; **177** (tl) Roger K. Burnard, (m) Studio Ten, (bl) Tim Courlas, (br) Steve Lissau; **178** (l) Paul Brown, (r) EPA Documerica; **179** (tl) Skip Comer/Latent Image, (tr) Rich Bucurel, (bl) Michele Wigginton, (br) James Westwater; **180,** Janet Adams; **181** (t) Skip Comer/Latent Image, (b) Studio Productions; **183** (tl) Larry Hamill, (tr) Hickson-Bender Photography, (bl) Thomas Pantages, (br) Ted Rice; **184,** George Anderson/ICOM; **186,** Michael Collier; **187** (t) Bruce Wellman/Tom Stack & Associates, (m) Ad Image